THE
PRIVATIZATION
BOOK

Harvey Goldman
and
Sandra Mokuvos

THE PRIVATIZATION BOOK

Harvey Goldman
and
Sandra Mokuvos

Acknowledgements

Throughout this book we speak of privatization as "a relatively new concept in the financing of wastewater treatment facilities." Indeed the concept is relatively new, but a number of pioneering communities and innovative private sector firms have enthusiastically accepted and pursued privatization as a viable and worthwhile undertaking. The knowledge and insights contained in this book would not have been possible without these pioneers. Without their foresight and creative thinking, privatization would not be the promising alternative it is today.

A number of individuals assisted in the preparation of *The Privatization Book*. We gratefully acknowledge the assistance provided to us by the professionals currently involved in privatization transactions, who took the time to review drafts of the book, and provide us with comments and insights based on their privatization experiences: Norm Brandel, Budget Examiner, Office of Management and Budget; Robert M. Davidson, Senior Vice President, The Parsons Corp.; Brenda S. Davis, formerly Assistant to the Commissioner, New Jersey Department of Environmental Protection, presently, Principal, Chambers Associates; Stacey Morse, Vice President, Shearson Lehman/American Express, Inc.; Personnel at the Office of Water Program Operations, U.S. Environmental Protection Agency; Benjamin M. Rawls, President, Engineering Design and Program Management Group, Research-Cottrell Inc.; David Saltiel, Partner, Nutter, McClennen & Fish; and Larry Silverman, Executive Director, American Clean Water Association (ACWA). A number of organizations have provided ACWA with financial support to assist in privatization educational activities, including a series of seminars at which *The Privatization Book* will be used as an educational tool. These firms and organizations are: Allied Engineers, Inc.; American Consulting Engineers Council; Betz Converse Murdoch, Inc.; Metcalf & Eddy, Inc.; Turnkey Services Inc.; and Zimpro, Inc.

Special thanks go to David J. McGrath, Publisher, and others at Engineering News-Record magazine for their interest in privatization and their willingness to co-sponsor seminars which helped to launch the public visibility of the privatization concept.

Special thanks also go to individuals at Arthur Young who provided their expertise in the areas of tax, financing, environmental and public sector management. While many individuals contributed ideas, the authors are particularly grateful for the extensive involvement of: Bruce M. Greenwald; Pat Krisher; John F. Laezza; David Mackenzie; and George A. Raftelis.

Sincere appreciation goes to Laurieann Daly and Camille Demonte for their production support.

New York City, NY
July, 1984

Dedicated to the
memory of my father,
Morris J. Goldman.
                    HJG

To the pioneers of privatization
Harvey J. Goldman
Sandra Mokuvos

                              To Arnie Bellush
                                    SM

Table of Contents

Charts and Figures

Preface

Environmental consciousness led to the creation of the United States Environmental Protection Agency in the early 1970s. Public demands for clean water, clean air and proper disposal of waste are among the calls to which Congress responded in establishing the EPA. The Agency was created in a period of Federal Budget surplus. Clean water funding was a national top priority and funds flowed to communities in need of facilities. Although clean water funding is still a priority, the financing challenge has emerged in the 1980s as the number one obstacle to clean water and a safer environment.

It is currently estimated that over $200 billion is needed to develop water and wastewater treatment systems in more than 5,000 communities. (1) While grants and local bonding used to be reliable sources to fund facilities, this is no longer the case. Needs have clearly outgrown the capabilities of governmental units. Consider the trends and events that have surfaced over the last decade:

At federal and state government levels:

- As part of the effort to reduce deficit spending and balance budgets, grant and aid programs have been severely reduced. When such programs are available, reduced funding eligibilities and long waiting lines are common.
- Tougher new standards of treatment have been promulgated for water quality and environmental safety. These have increased facility construction and operating costs.
- Enforcement programs, including monetary fines, moratoriums on community growth and other penalties, are being conceived and applied with increasing frequency to violators of environmental regulations.

At the local level:

- The historic practice of deferring maintenance on capital-intensive facilities is contributing to a national ''infrastructure crisis''.
- In too many locations, water and wastewater systems are in serious disrepair.
- Without some source of financial aid, the cost of constructing, rehabilitating or expanding facilities either draws down or exceeds limited local debt capacity and results in politically and economically unacceptable user charges.

The collective impact of these trends has been truly significant. In December, 1982, the National League of Cities and the U.S. Conference of Mayors undertook a survey of over 800 communities to identify the capital priorities, needs, and capabilities of local governments. Tables on the following page highlight survey responses.

The privatization concept was developed by Arthur Young and proposed as one of the potential solutions to the clean water funding dilemma. As used in the proprietary AY/Privatization® methodology, privatization is a process through which local governments can capitalize on advantages unique to the private sector in owning, building and/or operating capital-intensive facilities. These advantages may be significant when compared to facilities funded, built and operated by the public sector. Throughout this book, various terms are used to refer to the public sector. These terms include: municipality, community, local governing unit, city, state, etc. Privatization is applicable at all levels of government.

The advantages of service delivery through privatization include potential construction cost savings and lower financing costs because of tax benefits. Such benefits include items available on all business investments by taxpaying entities, as well as specific incentives provided by law, to encourage private investment in facilities that improve the quality of our environment. Other advantages include the opportunity for creativity in the arrangement of financing, and flexibility and economic advantages in the construction and operation of facilities.

In a properly structured privatization transaction, a public/private partnership is formed. This partnership is based on the premise that government should provide, but not necessarily produce, needed services. Characteristics and elements of these partnerships include:

RESPONSES TO INFRASTRUCTURE SURVEY
CONDITION OF PUBLIC FACILITIES

TYPE OF FACILITY	WATER STORAGE	WATER TREATMENT	WATER DISTRIBUTION	WASTE-WATER TREATMENT	SEWAGE COLLECTION	STORM WATER COLLECTION, DRAINAGE
% responding facility in good condition	54.8	50.6	46.4	37.2	36.2	23.9
% responding facility in need of repair	7.5	5.7	13.5	9.9	16.6	24.4
% responding facility in need of rehabilitation	8.0	6.7	14.0	17.4	28.3	31.9
% responding facility in need of replacement	3.2	4.2	3.9	7.4	4.9	11.1

NOTE: A number of individuals surveyed did not respond; percentages, therefore, do not sum to 100.

ABILITY TO FINANCE

TYPE OF FACILITY	WATER STORAGE	WATER DISTRIBUTION	WASTE-WATER TREATMENT	SEWAGE COLLECTION	STORM WATER COLLECTION, DRAINAGE	SOLID WASTE DISPOSAL, RESOURCE RECOVERY
% could use own resources	53.4	57.8	16.7	41.3	41.8	33.2
% need help	18.2	17.8	54.5	44.1	48.3	23.8
% "isn't in the budget"	17.3	15.1	20.8	9.6	5.0	29.2

SOURCE: Nation's Cities Weekly — April 25, 1983

- Ultimate users of the service provided by the facility should experience lower service charges than if the service was funded through conventional public financing approaches. In many cases, the user charges could approximate those resulting from grant-funded facilities.

- Most privatization transactions will not be regulated by public utility commissions; rather, safeguards to protect the public will be established through other vehicles, such as the service agreement between a municipality and the privatizer.

- All parties to the transaction must understand the risks involved, and take collective steps to ensure that risks are properly managed and reduced, and taken on by the party best-suited to bear them.

- Interests of concerned local groups, such as existing employees, vendors, system users and others, should be carefully addressed.

- The private sector partner should earn a favorable return on the investment. There should, however, be checks and balances in the service contract to ensure the fiscal integrity of the project, including verification that adequate monies are available for facility operation, preventive maintenance, eventual facility rehabilitation, and potential emergencies.

- The structure of the financial arrangements should include planning and accommodation for eventual ownership of the facility, if desired, by the local government. The financial mechanism to accomplish this must include due recognition of applicable tax and regulatory guidelines; it should ensure the avoidance of any financial burden to the public, and should not cause disruption in the user fee schedule.

Public/private partnerships are an emerging form of providing services to the public. The privatization concept is based on establishing an ongoing, long-term service, not a one-time sale. Therefore, privatization relationships must be established as partnerships, and are not right for everyone. These partnerships require a considerable degree of effort to implement, and place the elements of control in more hands than usual. Privatization partnerships are based on significant economic advantages to both sides, but the foundation of the transaction is the spirit of trust and cooperation between business and government.

A combination of economic, political, attitudinal and legal factors will contribute to the feasibility of privatization. Once determined to be feasible for a specific project, the implementation must be orderly and controlled. In this book, we present a process to determine feasibility and a step-by-step approach to implementation.

Tax law directly affects privatization transactions, although the transactions must have economic merit separate and apart from tax considerations. The recently enacted Deficit Reduction Act of 1984 impacts privatization transactions in several dimensions: it modifies certain of the depreciation benefits; it places limitations on the issuance of tax-exempt debt, including industrial development bonds; it limits arbitrage earnings; and it establishes criteria for service contracts. The collective impact of the changes in the 1984 Act is viewed by many as a clarification of the privatization approach and the economic benefits which are achievable by utilizing the concept.

Since Arthur Young first conceived and developed the privatization concept for treatment facilities, interest in privatization has grown significantly. Requests for speeches, presentations and articles have been overwhelming. Over the last few years, Arthur Young personnel have worked with numerous organizations and individuals interested in learning, contributing their expertise, and assisting to foster the birth and growth of privatization. We have also had opportunities to assist in evaluating and implementing various privatization transactions in the fields of water, wastewater, resource recovery and other areas. Through this book, it is now our privilege to transfer much of what we have learned to others.

Notes

(1) *Rebuilding America's Vital Public Facilities*, The Labor-Management Group, October, 1983.

1 INTRODUCTION

Recognizing that privatization is a relatively new concept in this country, it should be noted that any change from traditional methods to new approaches such as privatization must be handled carefully. A new approach must be fully understood with respect to its advantages, applicability and impact before its implementation can be seriously considered. Only after an approach has become understood and shown to be both feasible and desirable should the next logical step, implementation, be taken.

A certain amount of information is needed to evaluate and successfully implement a privatization approach. This book provides an in-depth understanding of the concept, of the issues to be addressed in determining project-specific feasibility, and of the basic elements to be included in an implementation plan. The book also presents privatization from the perspectives of both the public and private sectors as they approach a privatization opportunity.

Privatization has successfully been used abroad and by a few pioneering communities in the United States. The first wastewater treatment privatization transaction in the United States, for a 5 million gallon per day facility for Chandler, Arizona, was recently completed. Chandler, 25 miles southeast of Phoenix, is experiencing a tremendous population explosion fueled by the influx of the computer and electronics industry. The City's consulting engineer had designed a new sewage facility, but Chandler found itself in a position familiar to many other communities across the country. The City was so low on the Environmental Protection Agency's Construction Grants priority list that there was no funding in sight. For Chandler, the answer was private financing. Some $23 million in Industrial Development Bonds were issued in December, 1983, by the

1

City "to finance costs of the acquisition, design, construction, equipping and installation by Parsons Municipal Services, Inc., . . . of a facility for wastewater treatment."(1)

A number of pioneering communities across the country have expressed an interest in privatization, as indicated by advertised requests for qualifications and proposals (RFQs and RFPs) to privatize facilities. These communities are showing courage and initiative. Paving the way has required time and effort to put together detailed proposals and contracts. Many of the lessons learned by both the public and private sectors through these first efforts have been incorporated into this text. However, there is still a steep learning curve for privatization and much room for abuse. If the first few privatization projects are not properly planned and executed, privatization will not mature into a recognized, legitimate financing alternative.

Private ownership concepts have been used successfully in other fields to finance infrastructure projects. One example, private water companies, has been in existence for decades. Privatization concepts have also been used in the financing of resource recovery projects. However, privatization of wastewater treatment facilities is different. The decade of the 1970s taught communities and their advisors to rely on federal and state monies to subsidize local projects. Grant funding was the norm, although some local projects were undertaken without federal and state aid. Privatization is a definite change from the traditional methods of financing clean water.

The economic justification of privatization is rooted in the private sector's ability to combine factors such as construction savings, financing flexibility, operational advantages and tax benefits into a project. While the magnitude of the benefits will be project specific, in general, privatization enables the private sector to pursue a legitimate business opportunity and provide the public with needed services at an extremely competitive price.

The savings on a particular project will vary according to site-specific circumstances, such as the nature of the project, the financing approach used, and other items discussed in the text. Even in cases where the savings are below the norm, privatization may be appropriate due to a need for timely delivery of services, or a limitation on local debt capacity. Because privatization transactions typically would use Industrial Development Revenue Bonds or other forms of project debt, the debt incurred is not considered part of the community's outstanding indebtedness for statutory purposes.

PRIVATIZATION COMES TO NATIONAL ATTENTION

Arthur Young conducted its first, preliminary studies of the privatization concept for the New Jersey Department of Environmental Protection (NJDEP) in 1981. The initial study was designed to explore the viability of the privatization concept to help meet the state's significant funding need for facilities. Among the study conclusions were the following four key points:

1. *Privatization is Economically Viable:* In the absence of grant funding, a properly structured privatization transaction may be the most cost effective alternative available to a local community. In most cases, the economics of privatization should compare favorably to the economics of grant funding.

2. *The Private Sector is Enthusiastic About the Concept:* This conclusion has been substantiated in the cases where requests for privatization qualifications and proposals have been formally advertised. Typically, the number of responses from private sector groups has been greater than anticipated.

3. *Enabling Legislation is Required:* To create an environment conducive to privatization, state enabling legislation is often required. In "home-rule" states and certain other areas, privatization may take place without clarification of, or changes to, state laws. However, a thorough review of key statutes and regulations should be performed in any privatization effort. In states with a high degree of control over local affairs, such as New Jersey, procurement and public contracting laws are among the key factors which need to be addressed in enabling legislation.

4. *Public Education is Essential:* Political leaders and other key personnel representing community interests need to be educated about the advantages of privatization, how it works, the rewards to expect, and the possible risks which must be identified, minimized and, if possible, eliminated.

A number of events that took place shortly after Arthur Young's report for NJDEP was issued in June, 1982, thrust the privatization concept into the public eye. In August, the Association of State and Interstate Water Pollution Control Administrators (ASIWPCA) asked for a presentation on privatization at its annual meeting. ASIWPCA is an organization whose membership is comprised, among others, of the water division directors of every state. That presentation was given national press coverage in *Engineering News-Record*. A few months later, the theme for *ENR*'s annual water issue was "financing for clean water," and privatization was covered in depth. In mid-November the National Water Symposium was held in Washington, D.C. The sponsors, thirteen key trade groups and associations of the water and wastewater industry, requested a presentation on privatization (2). The thirteen organizations sponsoring the symposium are shown in Figure I-1.

The introduction to the executive summary of the conference proceedings states that the nation's existing water facilities are in a state of disrepair and deterioration, requiring major repair and reconstruction. "The greatest challenge is financing the improvements, not building them." The proceedings from the conference concluded that private sector involvement in the ownership and operation of needed facilities was an important concept for the group to support.

The national press has proven that it can play a very important role in the privatization education process. Recent articles have provided readers with excellent overviews of the concept and how it works. (3) In the fall of 1983, Arthur Young conducted the first series of privatization seminars across the country in conjunction with *McGraw-Hill's Engineering News-Record* magazine to educate representatives of the public and private sectors about the many aspects of privatization. The many other privatization seminars that have since been held are a good indication of the concept's growing acceptance.

Another important group that focused attention on privatization was the President's Private Sector Survey on Cost Control (PPSSCC). The task force reviewing federal construction management practices selected Arthur Young to investigate the potential savings that could be realized through privatization of wastewater treatment facilities. One of the task force's recommendations was that "Privatization of municipal wastewater treatment facilities must be encouraged and utilized to its fullest potential, thereby reducing state and local dependence on federal dollars." (4)

SPONSORS OF THE NATIONAL WATER SYMPOSIUM
ENDORSING THE PRIVATIZATION CONCEPT

- American Consulting Engineers Council

- American Public Works Association

- American Society of Civil Engineers

- National Society of Professional Engineers

- Water Pollution Control Federation

- Council of State Governments

- International City Management Association

- Municipal Finance Officers Association

- National Association of Counties

- National Conference of State Legislatures

- National Governors' Association

- National League of Cities

- U.S. Conference of Mayors

Figure I-1

State and local interest in privatization has blossomed as well. Arthur Young personnel have honored requests for privatization presentations from city and county governments, governors and their cabinets, state departments of environmental protection, governors' task forces on infrastructure financing, the U.S. Conference of Mayors, leagues of state legislatures, municipalities, cities and counties, and associations of water and wastewater authorities.

We are witnessing the inception of privatization in the wastewater treatment industry and further expansion of the concept into the areas of water supply, resource recovery and other capital intensive service needs of the public sector. As more projects are realized, privatization will be easier to carry out, because precedent setting, model transactions will be available for others to modify to fit local needs. The initial privatization projects must be undertaken carefully and intelligently. The first project in a particular state requires significant legal, institutional and regulatory involvement. Thorough analysis cannot be sacrificed for speedy and haphazard implementation. Circumvention of laws or of prudent management techniques should not be tolerated. Expertise in privatization will grow with time, as publicly available resources are developed and put to use. This book is a start. It incorporates the insights and experiences of "privatization vendors," professional advisors and municipal leaders, who already have been involved in planning and implementing privatization transactions. The sharing of knowledge and experience is essential as the concept has the potential to be of great benefit to both business and government.

In this book, we approach privatization from both sides of the privatization partnership. Whether privatization is first suggested for a project by the community or by an interested private sector firm, an organized approach to the feasibility analysis, implementation program and community oversight role during operation is essential. A recommended approach is presented in this book.

After the introduction and explanation of the privatization concept in Chapters I and II, the AY/Privatization® methodology is introduced in Chapter III. The four stages of the approach are analysis, decision-making, procurement and implementation. The privatization analysis is performed to determine the feasibility and project-specific nuances of privatization for a specific community. Generally, there are seven key areas in the analysis stage that need to be studied to determine the feasibility of privatization: 1) treatment needs; 2) available technologies; 3) degree of private sector interest; 4) the risks and benefits; 5) economic feasibility and financing approaches; 6) legal issues; and 7) regulatory issues, including the role of state government.

Once the seven key areas have been studied, and assuming that the feasibility and economic desirability of privatization is determined, one moves on to the next three stages of privatization. In the second stage, decision-making, the parties considering privatization must make a number of decisions related to the privatization objective, to the interests of the groups involved and to the establishment of a system of checks and balances over all project phases. The third stage is procurement, which includes all the steps involved in determining the parties to be involved in the transaction. The fourth stage, implementation, is based on the decisions made by the parties in stage two and the actions agreed upon in stage three. Successful implementation requires that two principal objectives be met: financial benefit must be achieved in a manner which protects the public's interests, and at the same time, economic incentives for the private firm must be established. The four stages are discussed in detail in Chapters II and III.

The remaining chapters are devoted to providing guidance to those who seek to implement privatization transactions. Chapter IV deals with the private sector's interest in privatization projects and discusses ways in which the private sector is likely to pursue privatization opportunities. Chapter V discusses the risks in a privatization transaction compared to traditional ways of implementing projects, and suggests approaches to managing those risks. Economic feasibility and the financing of a privatization transaction are the subject of Chapter VI. Legal issues are presented in Chapter VII, including a selected review of state legislation which may be required and of enabling legislation which has been introduced and passed to date. Regulatory issues and the role of federal and state governments in the development of privatization projects are presented in Chapter VIII. In our Conclusion we discuss the importance of the spirit of partnership, which is essential to the success of privatization, and outline the skills which are necessary to structure the privatization transaction. Appendices at the end of the book contain a discussion of the tax issues related to privatization and copies of selected privatization legislation.

Notes

(1)   From the Official Offering Statement of The Industrial Development Authority of the City of Chandler, Arizona, dated December 30, 1983.

(2)   *"Privatization of Capital-Intensive Infrastructure Facilities,"* presented by Harvey Goldman, Partner, Arthur Young & Company, at the National Water Symposium, Washington, D.C., November 17-19, 1982.

(3)   Recent articles about privatization, written by Arthur Young personnel include:

Water/Engineering and Management	*August 1982*
Constructor	*February 1983*
The Military Engineer	*June 1983*
Southwest & Texas Waterworks Journal	*June 1983*
Consulting Engineer	*January 1984*
American City & County	*March 1984*

(4)   *Report on Federal Construction Management,* President's Private Sector Survey on Cost Control, Spring-Fall 1983.

II THE PRIVATIZATION CONCEPT

"The need for new methods of public sector capital formation is now widely understood. And the search is on for methods which are creative, innovative, different, applicable to new and changing circumstances and which entail joint efforts by the public and private sectors."

Harrison J. Goldin
Comptroller
City of New York

Methods of financing environmental facilities will continue to evolve as leaders of business and government work both independently and together. Many believe that we are witnessing the increased transfer of financial responsibility for needed facilities from the federal government to state and local governments. Creativity by public officials and their advisors has resulted in concepts such as Infrastructure Banks, low-cost loan programs and loan guarantees.

Privatization will take its place among these alternatives, and assuming political acceptability, could well be the most cost-effective form of service delivery. However, not all projects will be suitable for privatization, even if privatization is desired by the public sector.

Privatization is a partnership between the public and private sectors, and like all successful partnerships, it must be based on the sharing of benefits. Figure II-1 shows the structure of a typical privatization transaction.

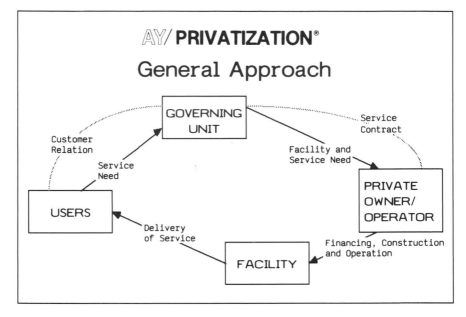

Figure II-1

The diagram illustrates several of the key relationships:

- From the governmental perspective, the government has a contractual relationship with a private owner/operator for the establishment and operation of a facility to meet the service needs of the area. In return, the community pays a service fee according to a predetermined rate structure, but the private owner/operator must meet contractually defined service standards to earn the fee. The public has numerous mechanisms to protect its interests, such as contracts for fixed service rates with previously agreed upon methods to determine increases.

- From the private owner/operator perspective, the owner/operator wins the business opportunity for an important service contract. In return for what is expected to be a satisfactory profit, the owner/operator assumes most of the risks involved in financing, constructing and operating the facility in accordance with contract terms for the delivery of the service.

- To the users of the service, the privatization transaction is invisible. The city sets the user charge rate and "retails" the treatment service, which is provided by the private sector "wholesaler". In addition to billing and collection from the system users, the city typically will maintain responsibility for system hookups and disconnections, customer correspondence and other customer interactions. The privatizer may be free to deal directly with non-municipal users of the system, and large commercial and industrial users within the local area.

- The city management has no direct relationship to or economic interest in the treatment facility. The facility is managed and controlled by the private owner/operator. Furthermore, the owner has the responsibility for repairs and replacements, and has the economic interest in the residual value of the facility after the service contract expires. The city, however, typically would have the right to buy the facility at fair market value in specified future periods.

Under this "general approach" private owners and operators of wastewater treatment plants can realize substantial tax benefits which supplement the construction and operating profits. These tax benefits are "shared" with the local government and the system users through service contract fees that are lower than those which would be required if the facility were established through public funding sources.

THE BENEFITS OF PRIVATIZATION

Privatization enables a community to meet its treatment needs on a timely basis. Many communities have no chance of obtaining a federal construction grant or state aid for a needed facility. Some eligible communities may face delays of several years before receiving grant funds. Others may find that even with a grant, reduced funding levels and more stringent eligibility requirements have made the local share of project costs so large that the project is still unaffordable. Compared to local financing, the economics of privatization should result in significantly lower user fees. Depending upon the nature of the system needed by a community, timing considerations, and the grant funding eligibility of that system, the economics of privatization, as measured in required user fees, may even be more advantageous than the economics of grant funding. Furthermore, by turning over construction and operation of a facility to a private firm, the community faces fewer risks associated with construction delays and facility performance.

Financing treatment needs through privatization has other direct advantages. Compared to federal grant funding, privatization minimizes federal and state involvement in local affairs, permits greater flexibility in sizing of treatment works and billing of users, and allows communities to avoid the indirect costs of grant administration and the potential headaches of grant audits. These and other advantages of privatization are summarized in Figure II-2.

There are also indirect advantages to privatization. One of the most significant is the timely economic development that may result. "Privatizing" a treatment facility creates a taxpaying, business entity in the community. In addition, increased capacity at the facility will, if desired, allow new industry to locate in the area, and developers to plan additional construction, thereby increasing the tax base.

Privatization relieves city administrators of facility and personnel management and O&M burdens while not diminishing their control over service cost and quality. The private operator is a "single point of responsibility" that city leaders can turn to for assured service. The responsibility of city leadership is to set and enforce service requirements; the responsibility to meet them—to manage the facility, deal with personnel matters, anticipate and resolve problems, interface with other interests—is the operator's. The operator, not the city, will bear the management and financial risks of not meeting cost or performance standards.

Another indirect advantage of privatization is related to financing. Some communities have chosen to issue general obligation debt or revenue bonds to finance treatment plants, or portions thereof, that do not receive federal funding. In many cases, there are state and/or local limits on the amount of debt a community can have outstanding at any one time. Privatization does not require a community to encumber its debt capacity. Even if Industrial Development Bonds (IDBs) are used to finance part of the project costs, because IDBs are backed by the revenues of the project and therefore not considered a general debt of the community, the community can retain its limited debt capacity for other essential services. In time, however, rating agencies may consider the community's long-term commitment in the service contract between the

**ADVANTAGES OF PRIVATIZATION
OF WASTEWATER TREATMENT FACILITIES**

- Provides a timely answer to environmental and economic development needs.

- Minimizes federal and state involvement in local affairs.

- Avoids construction time delays and compliance with federal procurement regulations, which collectively may increase the capital cost of a facility by 20% or more.

- Permits greater flexibility in factors such as sizing of treatment works and billing of users.

- Avoids indirect costs of grant administration and potential headaches of grant audits.

- Preserves local debt capacity for other essential purposes.

- May provide 100% of project funding, whereas grant programs only provide a percentage of costs and then only fund the "eligible" costs within that percentage. These costs are determined prior to when construction is undertaken, and the difference in costs caused by this time delay is often substantial.

- Privatization offers more predictability of costs because communities have a contractual commitment from their private sector partner in the transaction as to service provision costs.

- Proper operation and maintenance of facilities in many cases is best achieved through private sector contracting. Community difficulties may include the high pay scales necessary to attract and retain highly technical and well-trained individuals.

- In properly structured transactions, communities face fewer construction and operation risks.

Figure II-2

community and the private firm as an obligation which could affect the community's ability to borrow.

There is no question that there are economic benefits to privatization. The discussion above relates to the benefits afforded to communities that undertake privatization to meet their wastewater treatment needs. Private sector firms also receive benefits when they undertake privatization efforts. After all, the private sector is in business for profit. Both the public and private partners in a potential privatization project need to determine if the benefits outweigh the risks. In most cases they will, but the need for risk management, understanding what the risks are and how to deal with them, will still exist.

THE DEVELOPMENT OF PRIVATIZATION

A legitimizing precedent for private sector involvement in wastewater treatment in this country is the many privately owned water companies, even though they tend to be regulated public utilities as opposed to public/private partnerships. In Germany, public/private partnerships form basin-wide associations for the integrated management of both water and wastewater. These authorities, which first originated around the turn of the century, now have the authority to finance improvements and allocate and assess costs. In France, private companies provide a significant portion of public water and wastewater treatment services.

Privatization is not only applicable to wastewater treatment projects, but can be used for a wide variety of infrastructure needs. It is especially well-suited for equipment-intensive projects. These may offer greater potential savings than structurally-intensive facilities, because a higher degree of tax credits and tax deductions can be attained.(1) However, the financial feasibiltiy of privatization should be determined on a site-specific basis. In many cases, structurally intensive facilities have also proved to be worthwhile privatization opportunities for both the public and private sectors. (2)

Privatization is part of a trend of private sector involvement in what have traditionally been considered ''municipal responsibilities''. (3) Public officials are realizing that they do not need to produce services to provide them. These officials are recognizing that, through the private sector, they can have services delivered to their constituents in a timely and cost-effective manner. "Contracting out" is more efficient for a number of reasons, including:

- Competitive forces tend to drive inefficiency out of the market-place;
- Managerial and operational decisions can be made without the pressures of politics;
- The repercussions of decisions are felt directly by the decision-makers in terms of profits and losses. (1)

Contract operations of existing, publicly-owned facilities have been especially successful in the wastewater treatment industry. Many communities that had experienced difficulty in meeting effluent standards have turned to private operators to run their treatment plants.

Penalties for failing to meet strict effluent limitations, municipal inability to attract and retain qualified staff and the difficulties arising when existing personnel are required to operate equipment on which they are not adequately trained are among the factors that have encouraged communities to contract out services. In addition to offering highly qualified staff and on-going training programs, private firms operating more than one facility can realize economies of scale, which should be reflected in reduced user fees. Many public officials believe that an additional advantage of contract operations is that it is easier to control the performance of a vendor under contract than to control the performance of a public work force working under either union or Civil Service procedures.

With increased municipal reliance on the private sector and the success of contracting out in the wastewater treatment industry, the development of privatization was further triggered by cutbacks in federal funding and changes to the tax law. The combination of these factors led to the private sector's quick recognition of the business opportunity at hand.

THE CONSTRUCTION GRANTS PROGRAM

The U.S. Environmental Protection Agency's Construction Grants program must be discussed in terms of the nationwide need for wastewater treatment facilities and the 1981 amendments to the Clean Water Act, which reduce the levels of funding and limit the types of projects eligible for grant funding. In its 1982 Needs Survey, the U.S. EPA estimated that to meet the nation's wastewater treatment needs through the year 2000, approximately $118 billion would be required to pay for grant eligible portions of projects. (See Figure II-3.) Add to this the costs which are ineligible for grant funding and the needs of communities which are not on state priority lists (because their needs reflect growth and economic development which EPA does not fund), and the total dollar amount is even more staggering.

Currently, the Construction Grants program has an annual authorization of $2.4 billion through fiscal year 1985. Between fiscal 1984 and fiscal 2000, this annual level of authorizations would fall $80 billion short of the need for grant eligible costs. In addition, as of October 1, 1984, the 1981 amendments to the Clean Water Act reduce the federal funding share from 75% to 55% of eligible project costs, and restrict eligible categories to treatment systems, interceptors and correction of infiltration/inflow problems. Other categories remain eligible for grant funding, but to a much more limited degree. While these figures hold true as of the 1981 amendments, it should be noted that The Clean Water Act is up for reauthorization in 1984.

Cumulative federal funding for wastewater treatment since the 1972 Act was passed is approximately $35 billion. (5) There is still a $118 billion need. Privatization is not an alternative to the construction grants program; it is, at a minimum, a supplement to it. While privatization may not be the answer for all communities needing wastewater treatment systems, it is a viable solution for many of them.

PRIVATE SECTOR COST ADVANTAGES: TAX INCENTIVES AND CONSTRUCTION SAVINGS

Tax Incentives: In addition to the immense need for financing alternatives, privatization was sparked by the existence of the investment tax credit (ITC) and by changes to the tax laws which were made in the early 1980s. These changes, which make all capital investments, including privatization of water and wastewater treatment facilities especially attractive to the private sector, were made with enactment of the Economic Recovery Tax Act of 1981 and The Tax Equity and Fiscal Responsibility Act of 1982. The most significant aspect of these acts is the ability to depreciate equipment and machinery over five years and struc-

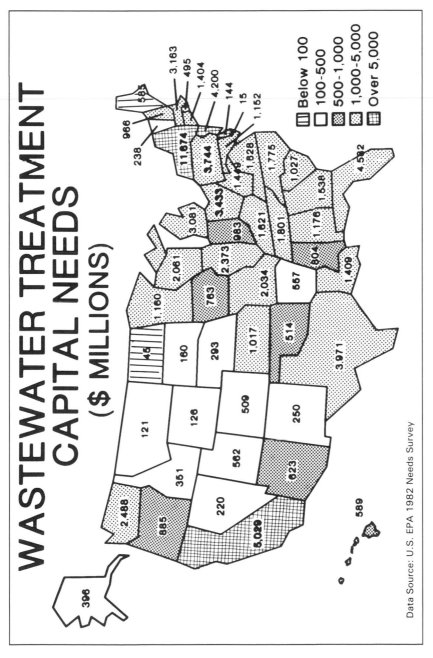

WASTEWATER TREATMENT CAPITAL NEEDS ($ MILLIONS)

Below 100
100-500
500-1,000
1,000-5,000
Over 5,000

Data Source: U.S. EPA 1982 Needs Survey

Figure II-3

tures over fifteen years, about half the time previously allowed. The most recent change in tax law extends the fifteen year period to eighteen years, but the change is insignificant with regard to the total available economic benefits. An overwhelming majority of the costs of a typical wastewater treatment plant are eligible for five year depreciation and the investment tax credit. The tax issues related to privatization are discussed in detail in Appendix A.

Along with accelerated depreciation and tax credits, the private sector can deduct interest payments if the project is financed with debt. Typically, debt financing encompasses the majority of the total project cost, with equity contributions providing the balance. Privatization provides especially attractive user fees when construction savings, operational efficiencies and tax benefits are combined with a relatively low interest cost, tax-exempt industrial development bond (IDB) to finance a facility. Using an IDB in privatization transactions is given more attention in Chapter VI.

Construction savings contribute to the private sector's ability to provide facilities at a lower cost. These savings vary according to site-specific circumstances such as the nature of the facilities needed, the construction time period and the manner in which the original cost estimates were prepared. From the privatization transactions and feasibility studies completed to date and from discussions held with professional consulting engineers, construction firms and municipal officials, it can conservatively be concluded that, compared to a treatment facility built through the Federal Construction Grants program, privatization can provide direct construction savings ranging from 5% to more than 20% of the treatment facility's total cost. These savings result from the private sector's ability to procure materials and proceed through design and construction in a more efficient manner and at a much faster rate than can municipalities.

The city of Carlisle, Pennsylvania, is a case where locally funded facilities were put in service in a much shorter time and at a much lower cost than if federal funds had been used. Needing a new wastewater treatment facility, and having been on a waiting list for a federal grant for some time, the City decided to take action. Using an innovative, low-load aeration technology for the plant design, the City built a 1 million gallon per day (mgd) facility in two years at a cost of $3.3 million. City officials estimate that, had they waited for a federal grant, the project would have taken five to eight years to complete at a cost of up to four times as much. In addition, they estimated that the annual charge per customer will be \$55 to \$65 a year less than if grant money had been involved.(6)

Delays due to federal and state procedural requirements are regarded by many construction industry observers as one of the major factors in the relatively high cost of public works construction as compared to private sector construction. A significant source of construction delays is in the pre-construction stage. The Office of the Inspector General of the U.S. EPA surveyed construction grant projects to which grants were awarded since 1976, and found that 634 projects, totaling nearly \$3.9 billion, had experienced pre-construction delays of more than 18 months. Twenty-two projects were delayed by more than four years. Four common reasons are cited for pre-construction delays. These include:

- Funding shortages at the state or local level
- Design changes
- Bid protests or citizens' lawsuits
- Site acquisition problems (7)

Delays which occur during construction also contribute to the high cost of projects. Having to conform to municipal procurement regulations can sometimes unduly stall projects if change orders are necessary. Public/private partnerships can be structured so as to minimize the delays and costs of change orders. Delays on U.S. EPA construction grant funded projects often occur due to required participation in time-consuming interim review and approval processes. Privatization does not include these costly processes.

THE ABILITY TO MOVE QUICKLY

There are a number of examples which demonstrate, through innovative approaches, how private sector involvement can quickly provide a community with a wastewater treatment facility. In one such example, a contractor and equipment manufacturer backed the construction of a .6 mgd, \$1.7 million advanced wastewater treatment plant for a housing development 25 miles southeast of Denver for the Castle Pines Metropolitan Water & Sanitation District in Castle Rock, Colorado. Construction was completed in nine months, and the fixed-price contract contained a three-year performance guarantee. The joint-venture backed construction for seven months with $700,000, and the remainder was financed with tax-free industrial development bonds sold by a public building authority.(8)

Operational efficiencies are viewed by many as another potential source of savings attributable to privatization. Using a business-like approach, the private sector will treat the provision of service as a product to be sold and profited from. Quality service at a lower cost will be sought through well-trained and experienced employees. While there are many cases of well-run municipal facilities, typically it is easier for the private sector to accommodate the pay scales necessary to attract and retain competent individuals. The talents of senior or specialized individuals can serve multiple facilities. Through this and other economies of scale realized when a private firm operates multiple facilities, such as centralizing administrative staffs and systems, ordering supplies in bulk and sharing common inventory items, operators and maintenance personnel, system users can realize further savings.

The private sector's relative flexibility, potential for tax benefits and business-like approach to service delivery can provide many advantages. However, oversight programs should be established to protect the public's interests. This subject is addressed in detail in the next chapter.

THE RESULT IS LOWER USER FEES

While there are distinct differences between the private and public approaches to the construction, ownership and operation of wastewater treatment facilities, the common objectives of the public/private partners should be identical. These objectives are to:

- Operate in compliance with applicable regulations and permits
- Operate as self-sustaining enterprises
- Minimize the economic burden to users (9)

In other words, the objective is clean water at an affordable price.

Even with its attractive combination of benefits, privatization typically is not a competitive approach when compared to the user fees for municipalities that received a 75% federal construction grant. (10) However, with lower federal grant funding levels, privatization, in some cases, can result in user fees that would be the equivalent to those charged if the community had received grant funds to construct all or part of the facility.

Figure II-4 compares a facility's user charges for a typical household under two different assumptions:

1. If the facility was 100% locally funded
2. If the facility was to be built, owned and operated under privatization.

The graph shows that full service privatization can be expected to result in significantly lower user fees than the local funding alternative. There are a number of factors that contribute to the user fee difference. They include the following:

- A properly planned privatization project may result in a construction cost savings.

- In a project where the "privatizing" group constructs, owns and operates the facility, the economic value of the tax benefits, on a present value basis, may approximate 25% to 30% of the project's capital cost.

- Through economies of scale and other factors, private operation and maintenance typically can be performed for no more, and in many cases for less, than a community could perform the services with its own employees.

- Through creative financings and management practices, rate subsidies and rate stabilization revenues can be established with greater flexibility through privatization.

While site-specific factors will influence the results of any one transaction, work to date has shown that a properly structured full-service privatization transaction has the potential to cut the debt service component of user fees anywhere from 15% to 40%, compared to conventional local government funding approaches without grant subsidies.

THE PUBLIC/PRIVATE RELATIONSHIP

The economics of privatization are driven by a number of factors, in-

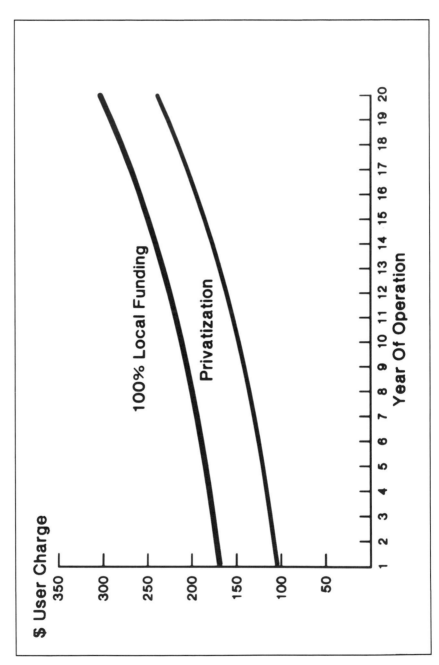

Figure II-4

cluding the financial transaction conceived by the private sector, the technology used in the facility (11), and most importantly, the relationship between the public and private sector.

There are currently a number of options for structuring the public/private relationship, and as more privatization projects are realized, other approaches will undoubtedly be developed. While variations exist, the two most common relationships that will occur between a community and the private sector are explained below.

Sale with Operating Contract (Figure II-5): In this approach a municipality designs and builds the facility, and enters into a service contract with the private sector for provision of the wastewater treatment service. The municipality sells the facility to the private sector firm, thus allowing the firm to claim depreciation and interest deductions. The property may also qualify for the Investment Tax Credit (ITC).

This approach may be suitable if the community wishes to contract, or has already contracted, for construction before becoming involved with privatization. It is also an appropriate method for refinancing an existing facility, if the facility was not originally funded with a federal grant. As explained in Chapter VIII, federally funded facilities are subject to the Office of Management & Budget's Circular A-102, which may require repayment of all or portions of the federal subsidy, from the proceeds of the sale. The Sale with Operating Contract approach can also be used in a situation where a community already has a wastewater treatment facility, built without federal funding, which needs to be rehabilitated or expanded. If the facility is not new, the ITC can only be claimed on the qualifying new process or system added by the private sector firm. Other tax benefits, such as depreciation and deduction of interest payments, can be claimed on the cost of the entire facility.

Full Service Approach (Figure II-6): In a full service approach, the private sector finances, designs, builds, owns and operates the treatment plant, and is eligible for all of the applicable tax benefits. This is an appropriate approach for a community that needs an entirely new facility.

This approach can also be used by a community in need of a new process for an existing facility. The Fallbrook Sanitary District, in Fallbrook, California, is considering this approach for such a case. In March, 1984, the District issued a Request for Qualifications for the financing, design, construction, construction management, start-up, testing, commissioning, operation and maintenance of an anaerobic sludge digestor

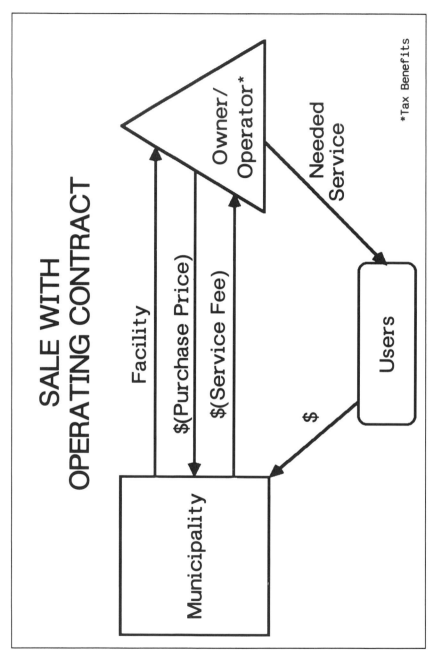

SALE WITH OPERATING CONTRACT

Owner/Operator*

Needed Service

Facility

$(Purchase Price)

$(Service Fee)

Users

$

Municipality

*Tax Benefits

Figure II-5

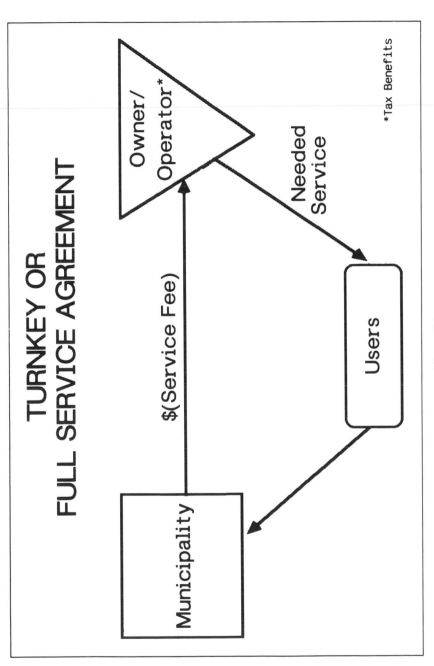

TURNKEY OR
FULL SERVICE AGREEMENT

Owner/
Operator*

Needed
Service

$(Service Fee)

Users

Municipality

*Tax Benefits

Figure II-6

to handle the solids from a 2.4 mgd activated sludge plant. Twenty-four firms or groups of firms responded to the request.

A METHODOLOGY IS A MUST

Structuring a privatization approach for a particular project requires a complete understanding of the privatization concept. Privatization is not based on complex ideas, but there are many issues to address in determining its feasibility and planning its implementation. To ensure the greatest probability of success, an orderly and controlled approach is needed to determine whether privatization is feasible and what form of the concept makes the most sense. Privatization must also be tailored to meet site-specific needs.

In the next chapter we present a methodology for a privatization approach. This methodology is the focal point of the text for examining and explaining the privatization concept from both the community and private sector perspectives.

Notes

(1)   Equipment-intensive technologies usually have a higher percentage of five year depreciable property, making the tax benefits of the transaction more attractive. Appendix A presents a more detailed description of the tax benefits available in privatization transactions.

(2)   Privatization has been found to be particularly attractive in the following areas: water treatment, storage and distribution; wastewater collection, treatment and disposal; biomass and resource recovery, biomass and solid waste to energy facilities; hydro-electric generation stations; criminal justice facilities; health and educational facilities; and transit systems. In addition, some communities and state governments have used privatization concepts to attract private investment for the development of publicly-owned properties not usable in their present condition, the conversion of vacant land into ratables and the rehabilitation of older structures. Parking garages and office space have also been developed through the privatization approach.

(3)   Choate, Pat, and Walter, Susan, *America in Ruins,* The Council of State Planning Agencies, 1981.

(4)   Savas, E.S., *Privatizing the Public Sector,* Chatham House Publishers, Inc., 1982.

(5)   Longest, Henry, *"The Federal Regulatory Perspective,"* Presentation at

the Arthur Young/*Engineering News-Record* Privatization Seminar, September/ October, 1983.

(6) Morrison, David, *"Pa. Town washes its hands of EPA to clean up waste," Philadelphia Inquirer,* August 30, 1982.

(7) *"Plant delays cost EPA millions," Engineering News-Record,* October 27, 1983.

(8) *"Sewage plant built in nine months," Engineering News-Record,* January 28, 1982.

(9) Arthur Young & Company, *Management Assistance Documents, Book 1 of 6, Management Challenges Facing Publicly-Owned Treatment Works,* May 1981.

(10) Historically, a federal grant has been for "eligible" project costs. In this analysis, it is assumed that all project costs are deemed eligible. In reality, the economics of privatization are likely to be relatively more attractive when grant funding of eligible costs is compared to privatization. In addition, when privatization of an entire treatment system, i.e., the collectors as well as the treatment plant, is considered, privatization becomes relatively more attractive because collectors usually are ineligible for grant funding.

(11) See note (1).

III | AN ORDERLY APPROACH FOR SUCCESS

*"Privatization comprises an alternative management
technique not just alternative financing."*

John M. Brusnighan
General Manager
Washington Suburban
Sanitary Commission

An organized plan must be established to determine if privatization is feasible and economically preferrable, and if so, to determine what specific form of transaction makes sense and how that transaction should be implemented.

An overview of the AY/Privatization® methodology is shown in Figure III-1. This systematic approach, modified as necessary to fit local circumstances, has been used in work with communities across the country. The elements of the systematic approach include a thorough fact-finding questionnaire, a series of computer programs to facilitate the evaluation of alternative financing and ownership structures, program pert charts to manage implementation and oversight activities, and a reference library of model laws, contracts, bidding documents and proposals.

The overall privatization methodology is comprised of four stages: feasibility analysis, decision-making, procurement and implementation. This chapter presents an overview of the methodology, including an

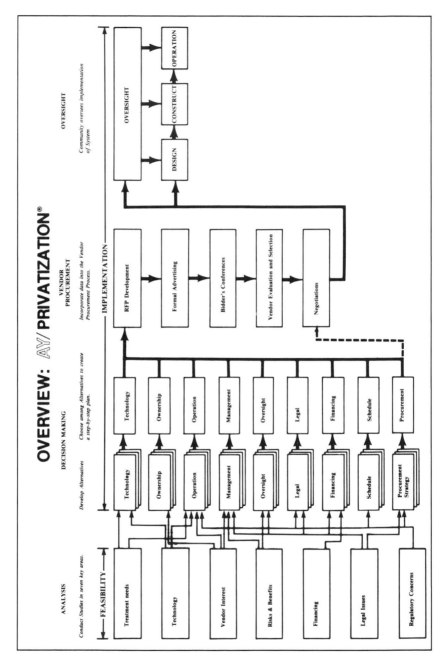

OVERVIEW: AV/ PRIVATIZATION®

ANALYSIS	DECISION MAKING	VENDOR PROCUREMENT	OVERSIGHT
Conduct Studies in seven key areas.	Develop Alternatives	Choose among Alternatives to create a step-by-step plan.	Incorporate data into the Vendor Procurement Process.	Community oversees implementation of System

FEASIBILITY — IMPLEMENTATION

Treatment needs
Technology
Vendor Interest
Risks & Benefits
Financing
Legal Issues
Regulatory Concerns

Technology
Ownership
Operation
Management
Oversight
Legal
Financing
Schedule
Procurement Strategy

Technology
Ownership
Operation
Management
Oversight
Legal
Financing
Schedule
Procurement

RFP Development
Formal Advertising
Bidder's Conferences
Vendor Evaluation and Selection
Negotiations

OVERSIGHT

DESIGN
CONSTRUCT
OPERATION

Figure III-1

introduction to the analysis stage and a discussion of the other three stages. The viability of privatization is dependent on more than just the economic feasibility of the concept. Determining whether privatization can meet a particular community's needs, while at the same time providing the private sector with a fair return on its investment, is a function of many interrelated variables. Regardless of potential economic benefits, communities are not going to accept an uncomfortable degree of risk in making commitments to or relying on "promises" from vendors. The public trust is too valuable to share with any except the most conscientious and capable vendor.

FEASIBILITY ANALYSIS

Seven key areas are studied during the feasibility analysis. If a different methodology is used, it should, at a minimum, include an analysis of the following seven areas:

Needs: Before a problem can be solved, it must be understood. In the case of privatization, the first step is to obtain a clear understanding of the community's needs. Many communities have this information at their fingertips. The need for a new wastewater treatment facility may be so great that the facility has already been designed and the only problem to overcome is a lack of financing. It is most likely that information pertaining to the community's needs can be obtained from the Mayor or City Manager, Public Works Director or Consulting Engineer. State and federal environmental agencies, regional planning councils and civic organizations can often provide additional insights.

Another good source of information is likely to be a 201 Facilities Plan, which may have been prepared as part of the United States Environmental Protection Agency Construction Grants Program process (1). However, 201 plans often allow for future population needs and assume a federal and/or state construction grant. Among the advantages of privatization is that a facility can be designed to meet immediate needs but not to immediately accommodate population growth over a 20-year planning horizon as is the typical case in grant-funded projects. The facilities can be "flow-matched" to achieve greater operating economics and modularly designed to facilitate future expansion. Even if the background information is abundant, local insights regarding needs should be obtained by working with local officials, employees and the community's engineer and other advisors.

The "needs" to which privatization may be applied could include:

- a total treatment system, i.e., plant and collectors
- components of a system, i.e., either the plant or collectors
- discreet new processes, e.g., sludge management facilities
- system expansions
- system upgrades and/or rehabilitation

Technologies: The range of technologies acceptable and available are determined and assessed as to their initial and life cycle costs, benefits, potential disadvantages, if any, and related factors. The choice of technology will affect the economic analysis in that the more equipment-intensive technologies will result in greater tax benefits. Equipment-intensive technologies offer a higher degree of five year depreciable property than do land-based technologies, increasing the tax benefits and potentially improving the economics of the transaction, assuming comparable or reasonably comparable capital costs. However, in making decisions related to technology, tax benefits should be secondary to process needs and sound engineering.

Once needs are determined, factors such as the use of acceptable, low cost "Innovative & Alternative" (I&A) technologies, time-phasing the construction of required capacity, and value engineering concepts should also be considered. The potential for revenue streams in addition to user fees, such as those obtained from the sale of residual materials or by-products should also be determined during the feasibility study.

Whereas I&A technologies were encouraged and to some extent financially guaranteed under the Environmental Protection Agency's Construction Grants Program, the use of these technologies in privatization transactions will most probably be evaluated on two major points:

1. The conditions under which a municipality and private investors will be willing to go forward with a technology which is not in widespread use; and

2. The I&A technology's apparent lower cost compared to the apparent higher degree of risk.

I&A technologies can be incorporated into privatization approaches, but it is reasonable to anticipate that greater emphasis will be placed on performance guarantees and warranties and other safeguards. And in most cases, the burden of providing performance guarantees will be on the organizations trying to sell the technologies.

The remaining feasibility study areas are treated in greater detail in subsequent chapters. However, the five other areas to be evaluated are introduced briefly below.

Vendor Interest: The level of private sector interest for privatization of a proposed project must be gauged, and a strategy to cultivate private sector interest in the proposed project may often be appropriate. One approach to encourage interest and competition is to advertise the proposed project and to request preliminary expressions of interest and/or qualifications. Preliminary meetings can be held with potential vendors to develop an understanding of the degree of interest and the areas of concern. As an example, before deciding to make the investment of time, effort and funds in preparing and issuing requests for privatization proposals, the Village of East Aurora, N.Y. decided to solicit preliminary expressions of interest from potential privatizers of a needed treatment facility. The total project construction costs were estimated at approximately $3 million. Armed with a strong demonstration of vendor interest for their project, the village proceeded with the confidence that potential privatizers would be available. Chapter IV, Vendor Interest, provides insights into the private sector perspective of privatization, including perspectives on the potential market and the business opportunity.

Risks & Benefits: Impacts on a site-specific basis must be addressed for each project from political, economic and social perspectives. These impacts are likely to include factors such as the impact upon economic growth and the control of future development. Equally important to consider are the strategy for protecting the interests of existing employees and local vendors, the potential of an increased tax base, and the importance of educating the public and the local press about the concept. Because privatization partnerships are a new form of transaction, both the risks and benefits must be clearly understood. In Chapter V, Risks, risk is considered a normal part of any capital intensive project, but an approach for identifying and managing the risks unique to the privatization concept is discussed.

Financing: To compare privatization adequately to other financing alternatives such as federal and state grants and local financing, one must understand how to structure a privatization project financing transaction that provides satisfactory returns to the private sector while maximizing the economic benefit to the community, in the form of reduced service fees. A variety of specialized professional skills and computer support tools are used to determine the financial viability of alternative privatization approaches and to structure the preferred form of transaction. Typical privatization transaction structures, such as limited partnerships and leveraged leases, (both are discussed in Chapter VI) should be considered.

Other issues may come into play during the economic and financial feasibility analysis. For example, the acquisition of existing facilities may be incorporated into the privatization approach. However, outstanding debt, related covenants and prior federal funding could negate the financial benefits of incorporating ownership of existing facilities. Other issues that may warrant early consideration are the potential mechanisms for ownership transfer of the facility from the private to the public sector at some point in the future. A more complete discussion of financial aspects of privatization appears in Chapter VI.

Legal Issues: A study of institutional factors addresses legal issues regarding procurement, construction, operation and other matters. State and local laws may influence various aspects of the transaction structure. It is also at this stage in the feasibility study that existing contracts with users and suppliers are reviewed for incorporation and/or modification with respect to the privatization approach. Representative legal issues and the typical contracts and related documentation which are needed in a privatization transaction are discussed in Chapter VII.

Regulatory Agency Issues: This area of study concerns the involvement of regulatory agencies at federal and state levels. Representative issues which must be addressed during the feasibility study are the role that the state government will assume with regard to privatization, compliance with National Pollution Discharge Elimination System permit requirements, enforcement issues, pretreatment program requirements, environmental aesthetics and other factors. The role of the state environmental regulatory agency, the public utility commission (or its equivalent) and other state agencies must be thoroughly understood. The federal and state roles in a privatization project are more fully explained in Chapter VIII.

The feasibility study is essential to determine if privatization is the most economically worthwhile alternative, to establish the feasibility of the concept with regard to local and state laws, and to identify any areas that need special attention if privatization is to meet the community's needs successfully. Upon completion of the feasibility study and the evaluation of the relative economic attractiveness of privatization, the community must decide if it will continue with the privatization process. If it chooses to do so, the community begins the second stage of privatization, Decision Making, and in so doing, undertakes the first steps of implementation.

DECISION MAKING

The feasibility study, if properly prepared, will have identified a variety of acceptable procedures or alternatives for each of the study areas. In general, there will be nine areas in which a community will have to evaluate different alternatives and choose among them to establish its step-by-step implementation plan. In some cases, circumstances may warrant that additional matters be considered. In others, previous decisions will reduce the alternatives to be considered. Some of the representative decisions to be made are addressed in the following paragraphs.

Technology: A community must decide which of the acceptable technologies available will be allowed under privatization. The community may want to limit the choices to those technologies that have especially attractive operating records. It may be that a community will decide that the wastewater treatment technology and plant design used in the 201 Facilities Plan is the only one that it would be willing to accept in a privatization plan. However, the community should remain somewhat flexible in this matter. If the potential privatizer or privatizing group includes an engineering firm, it may have ideas that would improve an existing design, or it may suggest design modifications or a lower cost, reliable technology that the community may not have previously considered.

Ownership: Decisions relating to ownership and operation of the facility are of special concern to both the public and the private sector, and critical to the way in which the privatization transaction is structured. For the private sector firm to be eligible for the tax benefits, it must have ownership of the facility. However, the public sector should have the right to a purchase option, due to various legal, financial and other matters. The purchase option is an important leverage factor for the public sector. The purchase option and the conditions under which it can be exercised must be written into the privatization contract. Through proper advance planning, ownership can be transferred to the public sector, after an initial period of private sector ownership, in a financially non-disruptive manner.

Other issues of ownership may involve the land on which the facility is located. It may be appropriate for the community to own the site and lease it to the private sector firm for a reasonable, annual fee. Ownership of existing facilities and variations in ownership of individual system components, such as public ownership of collectors with private ownership of the treatment system, should also be considered. Another ownership issue is the right of the initial owner to sell a project to other private interests.

Operation: The community must decide whether it has any objections to letting a private sector firm operate the facility once it is constructed. This decision must be made in light of a number of factors. For example, the private sector firm would only be eligible for the Investment Tax Credit if it has operating responsibility for the facility. If the municipality wishes to retain a significant portion of the direct operating responsibilities or to select an operator of its choice, there may be fewer vendors or different types of vendors, i.e., financial institutions, interested in the privatization opportunity. Many of the private sector groups which have expressed an interest in privatization transactions, have done so because of their interest in long-term operating contracts for the facilities.

Management: The private sector should always keep in mind that by undertaking privatization, a community is turning over provision of an essential service related to the public health. The nature and importance of the service demands that the community monitor the private sector's performance. In addition, most privatization transactions will include provisions for potential ownership transfer of the facility to the public sector at some future point in time. Since the public must be assured of the quality and reliability of the service provided and of the overall condition of the facility, the community should require that it be allowed to have significant quality control and oversight responsibility.

Direct management of the facility will most likely rest in the hands of the vendor. However, the municipality may want to stipulate minimum reporting and management system requirements which the vendor must meet. With the help of its engineers, employees and other advisors, the municipality can develop a monitoring program and take related steps to ensure that the facility is well run and properly maintained.

Oversight: Oversight responsibilities should include activities related to the design of the facility, and should continue through construction and operation. Although local officials will not be responsible for producing the service, they will be responsible for providing it. This means that public officials must concern themselves with the service quality, cost, and its timely delivery. In the case where a new facility is designed and constructed, the community's engineering advisors should review design plans and play a predetermined, ongoing oversight role during construction and/or operations. The role of the state department of environmental protection should also be defined in the privatization transaction. Discharge permit reviews and periodic facility inspections and/or audits should be conducted to ensure that the minimum acceptable requirements for operation and maintenance of the facility are being met.

Although these oversight activities will not be required until later in the privatization process, they should be designed and planned for in the decision making stage, and incorporated in the contracts and agreements of the privatization transaction.

Legal: If the feasibility study indicates that certain state or local laws prevent or are needed for privatization to occur, the community must plan accordingly to ensure legislative changes. This does not mean, however, that privatization plans must necessarily come to a halt until enabling legislation is passed. For example, in Auburn, Alabama, concurrent with its feasibility study and solicitation of vendor proposals, the community orchestrated activities to draft, have introduced, and create a constituency to support the enabling legislation.

Communities must also make decisions related to other legal and institutional issues. One such matter is that of existing employees in the municipality's public work force. Will it be legally possible for the municipal work force to be carefully blended with the private work force, so as not to jeopardize the tax benefits or other potential economies of private sector operational control? Typically, the answer is "yes." The compensation programs, retirement plans and other existing municipal benefits of the public work force are equally important to consider.

Financing: When a community makes the decision that privatization is desired, it decides that the benefits, as compared to other alternatives, are large enough to warrant the additional effort required to implement privatization.

As explained in Chapter VI, the structure of the financial transaction will directly affect the economics of the project. While estimates of the costs of service under privatization should be developed in the feasibility study, these should be recognized as preliminary in nature and, therefore, should be computed conservatively. It would be inappropriate for the community to not avail itself of the potential further cost savings that could result from private sector creativity or flexibility in establishing financing programs.

Schedule: Establishing a privatization schedule will require consideration of all aspects of privatization, including the immediacy of treatment needs and the means by which the services of the private sector will be obtained. Enabling legislation may be required before implementation can be achieved, but a community can proceed with a number of privatization activities contingent on the passage of the legislation. Reaching key milestones in the privatization process will enable the project to retain private sector interest and keep assistance at suitable levels.

A very important part of scheduling in the privatization approach is the inclusion of a public education program. While local officials considering privatization will have direct input from professional advisors, the general public will need some type of privatization orientation as well. The public education program can be a very formal one, including presentations with a question and answer period at town meetings. Another approach is to issue press releases related to milestone events, such as the community's hiring of a privatization consultant, the community's advertising for privatization proposals, or the signing of the privatization contract.

Perhaps the most comprehensive privatization feasibility study and implementation program performed to date has been in Norco, California. Norco is believed to be the first community in the country to undergo a "full service" privatization approach where one firm, the designer, will finance, construct, own and operate the privatized facility. The City of Norco has a population of 22,000 and has experienced significant recent growth. In addition, the expansion of the state highway system will inevitably lead to further development.

Metcalf & Eddy, Inc., Norco's consulting engineer and designer of a 3.2 mgd treatment system, was selected to develop the privatization plan to finance, construct, own and operate the facility. Scheduling for the privatization implementation program in Norco incorporates the development of a management program encompassing several dozen discreet task areas, with programmatic responsibilities divided among the community, Metcalf & Eddy, and respective professional advisors. An integral component of this schedule is a comprehensive public relations and public education program.

Procurement: One of the major challenges facing the community is selection of an appropriately qualified privatizer or service provider. Generally, if allowable under local and state law, a muncipality has two options for procurement: negotiated or competitive. In some instances a third option exists; a combination of negotiated and competitive. It may be feasible to structure a negotiated procurement for engineering or operating services with a competitive procurement for construction services or for the financing.

Typically, a negotiated procurement is less time-consuming than a competitive process, but the competitive process may offer the public sector greater control over the privatization contract with a wider range of transaction structure alternatives, and perhaps may even provide lower costs.

A negotiated procurement is likely to occur if a private firm has brought privatization to the attention of the community and sole source procurement is allowed under state and local law. However, because privatization is still a relatively new field, communities may be well-advised to use some degree of competitive procurement or independent, third-party review to seek the best contract available.

Competitive procurement may require more effort, but in the long run, it may offer the community the greatest advantages. A number of privatization opportunities have been presented to the private sector in this way. Figure III-2 shows reproductions of advertisements requesting privatization qualifications. In some cases it will be mandatory under state law or preferable under local options, to issue a Request for Qualifications (RFQ) first, pre-qualify or "short-list" a number of firms, and issue Requests for Proposals (RFP) only to those pre-qualified firms. Many public sector officials prefer this approach, because less time and effort are necessary to review detailed proposals. Furthermore, the cost of preparing a detailed RFP is deferred until proof of private sector interest is established. On the other hand, requesting qualifications and proposals at the same time reduces advertising costs and the time required to receive responses.

Without previous experience, one of the most time-consuming tasks of a competitive procurement is the preparation of the RFQ and RFP. A municipality may wish to hire an outside consultant to prepare the document, but even so, the research necessary to provide complete and up-to-date information will require that the consultant work with the municipality's internal and external personnel, including legal counsel and engineers.

Whether or not the RFQ is issued prior to the RFP, an RFP should still be developed as part of the competitive procurement process. The quality of the proposals received may be directly related to the quality of the RFP issued and the degree of effort expended by proposers in visiting with local leaders, gathering background data, and identifying alternative approaches for responses. The table of contents from a representative RFP for privatization of a wastewater treatment facility is shown in Figure III-3.

The aim of an RFP is to provide proposers with the information they will need to structure a privatization approach for a particular project. In addition, through the RFP the public sector can specify what it considers necessary to protect its interests, such as operational reporting and

REQUESTS FOR QUALIFICATIONS

Bayonne, New Jersey

The City of Bayonne requests a statement of qualification from interested firms who would finance, design, construct, own, operate and maintain an 11 (mgd) secondary treatment facility with or without the use of the existing primary treatment facility.

Interested firms (or groups of firms) should submit qualification statements which address the following:

1) Qualifications and experience of the firm(s) relevant to this project.

2) Qualifications and experience of key management and technical personnel who would be responsible for the project.

3) Preliminary concept(s) as to the firm(s) technical approach to reach required treatment levels.

4) Statement as to how project financing will be secured.

Please submit 10 copies of qualifications statements to: Mr. Marvin A. Eger, Business Administrator/Director of Finance, City of Bayonne, City Hall, Bayonne, NJ 07002.

Qualification statements must be received by 12:00 noon on November 30th 1983.

Arthur Young, the City's privatization consultant, will prepare evaluation criteria in reviewing qualification statements.

The City may prepare a list of qualified firms after evaluating the qualifying information and may invite them to submit formal proposals at a later date. The decision to accept or reject qualification statements shall be made by the City and its decision will be final. The City assumes no liability for costs incurred in responding to this request for qualifications or any subsequent proposal costs.

Source: ENR 10/6/83 p.111

State of Utah and Salt Lake City
Privatization of Wastewater Treatment Plants

The State of Utah, in conjunction with Salt Lake City, requests expressions of interest and statements of qualifications from firms interested in owning and operating wastewater treatment facilities in the State of Utah.

The State and the City have engaged Arthur Young & Company to determine the feasibility of privately financing wastewater treatment facilities. A privatization transaction would include: 1) Private financing; and 2) Project ownership and possible operation by private investors.

Salt Lake City has three specific projects which may be financed through privatization: 1) A proposed 16 MGD wastewater treatment plant to be considered for construction over the next 10 years; 2) An energy recovery process for an existing plant; and 3) A sludge management process.

In addition, the State of Utah has a number of communities, both rural and urban, with sewage treatment needs. The State and City desire to solicit expressions of interest and review the qualifications of firms interested in owning and operating wastewater treatment plants or related components. Please submit the following information: 1) A history of contract service experience in the sewage treatment area; 2) Financial resources of the firm available for privatization; 3) Description of company and personnel resources; 4) Specific segment of the wastewater treatment market most qualified to service, i.e., sludge management, energy recovery, treatment plants, etc.; and 5) Size of projects of interest to your company.

This is not a request for proposals. The State and the City will review your response in conjunction with the feasibility report prepared by Arthur Young & Company. Should the State or City desire to proceed with privatization, further steps for procurement of services will be determined.

Responses must be received by July 21, 1983 and should be directed to Mr. T. Craig Bott, Arthur Young & Company, 50 South Main, Suite # 1400, Salt Lake City, Utah 84144.

Source: ENR 7/7/83 p.53

Figure III-2

**REPRESENTATIVE RFP
WASTEWATER TREATMENT FACILITY**

TABLE OF CONTENTS

I. Letter of Welcome

- Summary of need and opportunity
- Community interest in privatization

II. Background Data on the Local Area

- Local demographics
- Economics
- Population trends

III. Technical Information

- Treatment needs
- Acceptable technological approaches
- Existing facility and plant site data
- User discharge data
- Permit and compliance standards
- Residual process materials

IV. Legal Information

- Customer, labor and supplier agreements
- Regulatory matters
- Guarantees and warranties
- Governing statutes
- Key contractual considerations
- Methodology to resolve unanticipated events

V. Financial Information

- Acceptable financing approaches
- Safeguard and transfer of existing investment
- Future investments, guarantees and warranties
- State and local tax information
- Considerations regarding user fees
- Sources of financial assistance

VI. Anticipated Interfaces

- Local community
- Regulatory community

VII. Facility Management System Requirements

- Construction management
- Operation and maintenance management
- Reporting and control systems

VIII. Other Sections, including

- Audit and control requirements
- Required qualifications of bidders
- Environmental and aesthetic specifications
- Schedule requirements
- Proposal format and contents
- Proposal evaluation and selection processes

Figure III-3

facility management system requirements. A thorough RFP should facilitate a timely, responsive proposal. Representative sections of a comprehensive RFP are discussed below:

Letter of Welcome: A summary of the privatization opportunity and the needs that are to be met should be presented. An indication of community interest and the general climate in the area toward privatization should be presented. Any past experiences that the community has had with contracting out or other privatization-related undertakings should also be presented to give potential proposers the incentive to expend effort in the proposal activity.

Background Data on the Local Area: RFPs should provide prospective vendors with information on local demographics, economics and population trends. This will enable proposers to prepare transaction assessments and to develop financial comparisons between their privatization approach versus existing user fees, as well as other financing alternatives. Population trends will allow future use estimates to be prepared, so that facility sizing and/or potential expansions can be incorporated into the approach. Future rate provisions can also be addressed with knowledge of the anticipated user base.

Technical Information: This section should contain a detailed description of treatment needs as required by applicable state and federal regulations, and of specific local conditions. The technologies which the public sector is willing to accept to meet these needs should also be addressed, if they have not already been addressed in an RFQ. Information on any existing facilities, plant site and water quality, or user discharge data should be presented with any other technical information, such as permit and compliance standards to be met, and descriptions of any residual process materials.

Legal Information: This section must be prepared with the aid of local legal counsel familiar with the governing laws and statutes of the area. Most of the information in this section will relate to existing contracts and the contractual considerations that should be included in the proposal. Additional information could relate to performance guarantees, operational warranties and other contractual terms and conditions.

Financial Information: It may be helpful to work with municipal financial advisors when preparing this section. This section should contain financial statements of the community, state and local tax information, other fiscal data and municipal considerations regarding user fees. If the project is to upgrade or replace an existing facility on which there is still outstanding debt, relevant information should be made available to the proposers. They, in turn, might be asked to present a plan which incorporates the existing facilities and the related debt. Any sources of financial assistance, such as the possible issuance of industrial development bonds, tax abatements or other incentives should also be included in this section.

Anticipated Interfaces: The anticipated interfaces, i.e., interactions between all the parties in the privatization project, should be discussed. These interfaces will require the coordination of the different municipal agencies with jurisdiction over parts of the project, and of state and federal agencies. In most cases, there will also be interaction between the users of the facility and the local government unit, possibly requiring a public relations program and an eventual customer service program.

Facility Management System Requirements: The requirements presented in this section are part of the public sector's oversight program. By requiring specific construction, operation and maintenance management systems, the public sector can establish a comprehensive system for monitoring performance, and thus place reporting responsibility on the shoulders of the private firm. Organized systems also allow the public sector to review and audit private sector performance on a timely basis.

The proposals being requested and the effort put into their development are especially important because they will be the base for privatization contract negotiations. Therefore, it would be appropriate to give potential bidders the opportunity to ask questions prior to submitting proposals, by holding a bidders' conference or scheduled pre-proposal meetings, ensuring that all potential vendors are treated in an equal fashion.

More importantly, the public sector must devote the required resources to evaluate and ensure complete understanding of the proposals received. The proposal evaluation team should be composed of individuals with the multi-disciplined talents to evaluate the material at hand and make proper comparisons between competing proposals. The City of Auburn, Alabama authorized issuance of an RFP in October, 1983 directed at private firms interested in financing, owning and operating a new 5.4 mgd wastewater treatment plant. A "blue ribbon" committee was appointed to evaluate the proposals. This committee, which had the task of evaluating eight proposals, was composed of three elected officials, the Chairman of the Industrial Development Board, a representative of the President of Auburn University, two attorneys, a leading expert in sanitary engineering from the Auburn University faculty, the City's auditor, the Associate Dean of the School of Veterinary Medicine, the City Manager, the Finance Director and the City Engineer. The City of Auburn was also assisted by an independent financial advisor.

Once a vendor is selected, contract negotiations based on the proposal can begin. Experience has shown that vendor selection and negotiation need not be two separate events. Auburn gave each of its eight proposers the opportunity to make a two-hour presentation to the evaluation committee. After the presentations, four proposers were chosen and sent a detailed list of questions regarding their proposed financial transaction. Two of these four firms were chosen as finalists and concurrent negotiations were undertaken with both, to determine which could provide Auburn with the most cost-effective privatization approach. While concurrent negotiations may not always be advisable, they should be considered by communities as a possible means to cost savings and other potential benefits. The privatization-enabling legislation proposed in the State of New Jersey, (see Appendix C), specifically suggests that communities may want to enter into concurrent negotiations.

In the negotiation process, both the public and private sectors need to remember that they are considering the establishment of a long-term partnership. Benefits need to be shared and responsibilities and risks need to be fairly allocated. Neither the public nor the private sector should agree to a contract that does not provide it with an equitable and worthwhile arrangement.

OVERSIGHT

Although oversight is the fourth stage of privatization, an oversight plan should be developed as part of Stage two, Decision Making. Actual implementation of the oversight plan takes place during design, construction and operation of the facility.

There are two reasons for community oversight. First, the community must be assured that the plant is operating and being maintained adequately, and that treatment service is being provided in a reliable manner. Second, the community may want to take ownership of the facility at some time in the future, and it should ensure that the plant will be in proper, well-maintained condition.

CONCLUSION

The methodology for determining the feasibility of and subsequently implementing a privatization approach need not be complex. However, it should be organized and thorough, including the involvement of appropriately qualified individuals. A well thought-out and coordinated effort, consistent with a community's goals and objectives, will provide a solid base from which to implement a successful privatization transaction.

Once the feasibility and desirability of privatization is established, policy decisions must be addressed and an implementation program should be established. The overriding objective of the implementation program is to secure the most cost-effective privatization project, in a manner designed to protect the public's interests while providing a reasonable financial return to the private sector. Equally important, education and awareness programs must be simultaneously established. Public attitudes and concerns regarding privatization must be addressed. Public officials will not go forward with a new concept unless they understand it and are comfortable with it. Regardless of the potential economic benefit, they must be confident of their ability to control the implementation, to insulate their constituents from risk, and to achieve a business relationship with partners they can trust.

Notes

(1)   Section 201 of the Clean Water Act requires that studies be done to assess existing conditions and the need for new wastewater treatment facilities across the country. The "201 Facilities Plan" for a community's area is the first step a community must take in obtaining a United States Environmental Protection

Agency Construction Grant. The 201 plans typically contain information related to conditions in the planning area, including existing wastewater flows and treatment facilities, demographic and economic projections, forecasts of future flows and solutions to the existing water pollution problems (including flow and waste reductions, pretreatment programs) and proposed costs and preliminary designs of new treatment facilities.

IV VENDOR INTEREST

There is no shortage of private sector firms interested in the business opportunity of owning and operating wastewater treatment facilities. In mid-1983, Camden, New Jersey, advertised what is believed to be the country's first request for privatization qualifications (RFQ) for wastewater treatment facilities. The RFQ sought interest from those firms seriously interested in owning and operating both a 17 million gallon per day (mgd) and a 75 mgd wastewater treatment facility. The City received replies from nineteen major designers, contractors and financial firms. Camden subsequently hired advisors to determine how and when it could go forward with the concept.

Camden's pursuers were matched in enthusiasm by groups which submitted qualifications statements or proposals to other municipalities interested in privatization. For example, in recent procurement solicitations:

- Salt Lake City and the State of Utah received 25 expressions of interest for various potential privatization projects.
- The City of Bayonne, New Jersey, received 15 qualification submittals in response to the need for an 11 mgd secondary treatment facility.
- The Fallbrook Sanitary District in Fallbrook, California, received 24 statements in response to a request for expressions of interest for privatization of a new sludge treatment facility.

Communities looking for assistance from the business community can expect to find willing partners, but not suprisingly, private sector interest may have to be cultivated. At the same time, while the privatization industry is resulting initially from publicly advertised requests for proposals, more and more business organizations are initiating programs to evaluate the concept and create public sector interest in its implementation.

Private sector interest in privatization is evident. A number of large design and contracting firms are stressing privatization in their annual reports to stockholders as a new business thrust area, as those firms begin to re-evaluate their roles in the water, wastewater, and waste management industries. At a privatization seminar in the fall of 1983, the president of a large engineering firm told a group of public officials and private sector representatives, "We view ourselves as a second-generation engineering firm specializing in engineering management. We can be the catalyst to help you obtain badly-needed facilities by arranging financing, and providing design, construction, and plant operations." Investment banking firms and other financing sources are also devoting resources to cultivating privatization opportunities.

This chapter highlights some of the major considerations for private firms that are attempting to penetrate the privatization market. The insights in this chapter will also provide local officials with a better understanding of the private sector's business interest in privatization opportunities. Included are discussions related to the following:

- The size of the potential market
- The resource recovery precedent
- Market entry
- The profit potential
- How opportunities are likely to be pursued

THE POTENTIAL MARKET

The potential market in the United States for privatization of water, wastewater treatment, and waste management services is, on either a relative or absolute basis, enormous. As mentioned in earlier chapters, estimates of the need for water and wastewater treatment systems exceed $200 billion. The number of communities which need investments in such systems is estimated to be greater than 5,000. A key question which potential "privatizers" will ask, however, is where and when will the market develop? While the need for wastewater treatment is spread throughout the country, a number of states, such as Utah, New Jersey,

Pennsylvania, Tennessee, California, Florida and Arizona have emerged as the apparent early fertile grounds for the concept. Insights regarding some of the actions which may be required to cultivate additional areas are discussed in Chapter VIII.

Where and when the true market will develop is anyone's guess. One fact, however, cannot be overlooked. Wherever they are and whoever is involved with them, the importance of successful pilot projects will have a lot to do with the pace at which the potential market develops and matures. Clearly, nothing will spur market development faster than pilot project success stories. Considering that the environmental industry is relatively close-knit and well organized in terms of trade groups and communication vehicles, news about the results of pilot projects can be expected to spread quickly. Equally close-knit are the associations of city managers and financial executives. In terms of project selection and project results, doing the first projects correctly is of utmost importance.

Looking at the communities that are undertaking privatization projects and the ways in which these projects are being initiated and carried out can provide significant insight regarding future privatization project sites. There appears to be a set of criteria for determining whether privatization will be successful in a particular community. The following factors will directly affect the community acceptance and success of a privatization project.

- The community needs and desires new or upgraded facilities: Regulatory agency pressure for a new and/or improved facility, combined with a sincere desire for the project on the part of the community, is an ideal set of circumstances.

- The community has little or no chance of receiving grant funding for the project: The economics of the privatization approach should prove to be, by far, the most cost-effective option for the service delivery needs of this community.

- The community has had favorable experience dealing with the private sector in the past: Favorable past experience with contract services in areas such as solid waste collection and disposal, snow removal, data processing, power supply, etc., should present a good background for a privatization transaction.

- The community has a full understanding of the privatization concept: This community should designate a top person as the leader of its privatization program.

- The community is prepared with its own set of engineering, legal and financial advisors: Community interests should be well-protected in the transaction, with all risks identified and properly managed.

- The privatization approach is well organized and a well thought-out implementation plan is established: A haphazard or incomplete approach to implementation may cause frustrating delays and have widespread negative results.

THE RESOURCE RECOVERY PRECEDENT

Although there are many areas served by private companies in the business of water supply, most tend to be regulated public utilities. Since privatization typically would not involve utility-type rate regulation by a state government agency, perhaps the closest parallel to wastewater privatization concepts is in the field of resource recovery, where facilities are used to convert solid waste to steam and/or electrical energy. Much can be learned about structuring and implementing public/private partnerships from resource recovery case histories. One must keep in mind, however, that while similarities do exist, there are several significant differences between privatization in the resource recovery field and the privatization of wastewater treatment facilities.

Based on experience in the field of resource recovery privatization, the following conclusions regarding privatization of wastewater treatment facilities can be reached:

- Wastewater privatization should be significantly easier to implement than resource recovery projects. The reasons include the following:
  1. Facility siting is typically a major problem in resource recovery; in wastewater, siting is often more easily accommodated and accepted by the public.
  2. Financing should be easier for wastewater, as the perceived technology risk is minimal compared to resource recovery and, typically, the cost for a project is less. This should make structuring the financing easier, and may open up financing options not possible in resource recovery projects. In addition, in resource recovery, the primary revenue is from energy sales to

a public utility. Such revenues are typically viewed by investors as a less secure income stream than the fees obtained from a local government and/or non-municipal users for processing wastewater.

3. "Capturing" access to the solid waste stream is often difficult in resource recovery, as agreements with various municipalities are often required. For wastewater projects, facilities are typically designed to a single area's needs and the collection system may already be in place.

- Successfully implemented resource recovery projects are good models to modify, as necessary, and fit to the project specifics of wastewater privatization projects. The "modeling", however, necessitates several major modifications (e.g., incorporating the concept of potential ownership transfer to the public sector in a financially non-disruptive manner, satisfying differences in project financing requirements, etc.).

For these and other reasons, the success of privatization projects in the field of resource recovery should serve as positive reinforcement to both the public and private sectors that wastewater privatization can be accomplished. And the lessons learned concerning the need for adequate planning, well-managed implementation and good public relations can be applied to help assure successful wastewater privatization development.

MARKET ENTRY

The privatization market is attractive to many private sector groups, including engineering firms, construction firms, equipment manufacturers, utility operators and others. Since the technology for wastewater projects is generally regarded as proven and stable, market entry poses no significant barriers to groups that can demonstrate the ability to design, construct, own and operate such projects. Clearly, the community's consulting engineer is already in an advisory role and may be in the position to both educate his client about privatization and to assist in guiding the evaluation and potential implementation of the privatization concept. Whether or not that engineering firm desires to be an owner or operator of the needed facility, there are engineering, construction management and inspection services, start-up activities and other professional services which will be needed if the project moves forward. The community's consulting engineer could be significantly involved in the process of implementing the privatization project, depending on factors such as the manner in which privatization is presented to the community for study and evaluation, community policy decisions and other matters which should be considered in the privatization feasibility study.

Those groups already offering contract operations services for wastewater facilities may have a significant head start, because those that have successfully tapped the market have earned the trust of municipalities. As the market matures, the successful groups will be those that take due care to structure orderly implementation programs, properly address public concerns, are content with reasonable profit levels and have pilot or demonstration projects to point to.

The last point is especially important, as public officials in need of projects are likely to ask potential privatizers, ''Where have you privatized a project before and who can I talk to from the community involved?'' Since the private sector recognizes the need for market positioning and early demonstrations of successful projects, it is generally expected that the first group of communities in the country, and certainly the first community in a particular state to adopt privatization, will receive a significant amount of competitive inquiry and proposals from the private sector. The benefits of being first, from the public perspective, should include receiving a very favorable set of economics in the transaction. The private sector may view its reduced benefits for the first project as a market investment.

PROFIT POTENTIAL

The profit potential in a privatization transaction must be attractive to the private sector. According to one prominent engineer, engineers ''can make a living owning and operating treatment plants.'' (1) A community must want its privatization partner to stay in business and, accordingly, must recognize its need for a reasonable profit in the transaction. The profit potential in the transaction is composed of the following representative elements:

- Engineering design fees

- Construction management fees
- Construction profits
- Operation and maintenance profits
- Financing profit
- Residual value of the facility after the debt is retired; and
- Opportunity to undertake supplemental investments, as needed, related to the project at hand or other elements of the community's treatment system.

The profit potential in a particular transaction will vary considerably depending upon how many different groups are involved and how the transaction is structured.

HOW OPPORTUNITIES ARE LIKELY TO BE PURSUED

While private sector firms will gear their approaches to privatization according to company-specific and site-specific circumstances, there are some generalizations that can be made about how privatization opportunities should be pursued. The following list, while not exhaustive, provides some insight:

- The privatization concept should be presented to local officials and local employees to ensure that, through proper education and mutual understanding, all concerns are carefully identified.
- If applicable, parallels can be drawn to other local situations in which privatization concepts have been used.
- Select a project where there is a real need.
- The support of the state government, especially that of the state department of environmental protection should be sought.
- A relationship with the community, based on trust and the sharing of potential mutual benefits, should be fostered.
- If the community has not already obtained professional advisors, the private firm should indicate the need to involve others who can assist the community. The community's negotiating team must be able to match the sophistication and experience of the privatizer's legal, financial, and other advisors.

- The private firm should have patience. Potential privatizers must realize that the process will take time. Public leaders will not want to rush into the transaction and may themselves be delayed by bureaucratic procedures, political considerations and compliance matters over which they have no direct control. Attempting to force-fit a privatization transaction into an artificially imposed time-frame will not pave the way to successful implementation.

Creating privatization opportunities requires a significant amount of up-front leg work, with no guarantees that the effort will result in a project. As privatization becomes a more widely-used approach, the up-front work will decrease significantly and private firms will find themselves reacting to requests for privatization qualifications and proposals more often than initiating opportunities. However, it is likely that those firms willing to invest the time and effort now will make themselves well known and, hopefully, well respected as the leaders in the privatization marketplace.

Notes

(1)   Davis, William K., Vice President, BCM Eastern, Inc., a subsidiary of Betz Converse Murdoch, Inc. Taken from *"Private cash in public pipes,"* *Engineering News-Record*, January 19, 1984.

V RISKS

Many believe that a properly structured privatization transaction will relieve a community of significant risks related to the construction costs, operations costs and operability of the treatment works. Such should be the case. For example, unlike the situation where it bears the risks of construction delays and cost overruns, the community can be protected by contractual agreements which put the burden of cost and schedule compliance on the privatizer. Furthermore, most privatization service contracts can be expected to protect the community from ineffective plant operations. If the desired and agreed upon level of treatment is not provided for reasons within the operator's control, the community should not be expected to pay for treatment costs. In such cases, the operator, rather than the community, should face the financial burden of state-imposed fines for failure to meet discharge permit standards. Furthermore, the community should have the right to replace the operator if operating problems, which should have been avoidable, continue to occur.

There will be a cost associated with passing construction and operations risks to the private sector, but the economics of privatization should allow the transaction to move forward in a manner through which everyone wins. The private sector is perhaps better able to manage and absorb certain risks. Every good business opportunity has some degree of risk. Successful businesses are those that have demonstrated the ability to perform and to manage risk.

This chapter addresses certain of the risks which must be addressed in a privatization transaction and provides insights from case histories as to how risk management was handled. It is important to recognize, however, that neither party in the transaction, business or government, should seek to put the other in an unacceptable posture vis-a-vis risks. If that situation results, or is viewed as emerging, the public/private partnership will not work over the long term. It may work for a limited time only, and then may have to be dissolved with potential embarrassment to all involved.

One needs to be protected from unacceptable risk, but one also needs to determine what risks are acceptable, and moreover, reasonable to assume, given the benefits which privatization affords to the public and the business community. For privatization to work, the proper attitude of the public/private partners is to seek to work together to:

- Identify the risks which must be addressed;
- Identify the consequences of those risks;
- Take prudent management steps to minimize the probability of the consequences occurring;
- Agree on actions to reduce and to allocate the risks, including allocation to third parties such as insurance companies.

A proper attitude is to seek a working relationship where positive guarantees are provided by each of the public/private partners. These positive guarantees will minimize risks and enhance the overall project. For example, the privatizer and the community should both recognize that potential bond buyers and/or equity investors will look to safeguard their investments. The greater the risk they perceive, the higher the financing cost of the project and the higher the resultant service fees. The community can make potential bond buyers less concerned about the repayment risk, if the community guarantees its long-term use of the treatment works, assuming proper operations, and further guarantees to provide a minimum level of usage. The community should recognize that it is not pledging its credit to the project. One of the key advantages of privatization is that it preserves the debt capacity and creditworthiness of the community.

The privatizer, in turn, would be expected to guarantee the successful operations of the treatment works, assuming certain ranges of influent quality and quantity, and assuming predetermined levels of treatment to be provided. Pushing the risks and guarantees one step further to protect the public/private partners, the plant operator could seek certain guarantees of the equipment suppliers and plant designer/constructor, while the community may impose sewer use ordinances and pretreatment requirements on dischargers to back up the community's guarantee as to quantity and quality of the influent to be treated.

With this cooperative spirit of working together to manage risk, the public/private partnership can come to fruition. The public and private sector partners must take the time to work together to identify the risks involved in the financing, construction and operation of the desired treatment project. Both parties must ensure that an acceptable risk management approach is conceived and implemented.

To some extent, the financing risks will be dependent on the financing approach selected for the project. A detailed discussion of project financing and the financial community's requirements to minimize construction and operating risks is presented in the next chapter. The remainder of this chapter focuses on the construction and operating risks as they may be perceived by the community and the privatizer. Such risks should be discussed and negotiated by the parties involved, with agreements incorporated into the service agreement and other privatization transaction documents, which are discussed in Chapter VII.

CONSTRUCTION AND OPERATING RISKS

Cost overruns, contract suspensions, unforeseen site problems, force majeure delays caused by ''acts of God'', such as fires, floods, and earthquakes, and inadequate insurance are typical construction risks. None, however, are specific to privatization. In a privatization approach, these construction risks, typically, should be directly faced by the project owner, not the community. But the community, as a partner in the transaction, should seek to be involved in the risk management program.

There are ways in which the community can require that the privatizer take measures to protect himself, and indirectly the community, from construction risks. For example, if the private sector firm designs the treatment facility, the community could have the designs reviewed by its staff or its consulting engineer. Once construction is under way, written progress reports against a pre-established project schedule should be prepared for the community. If the privatizing firm is using a facility design which was previously prepared by the community's design engineer, the privatizer should review the design, have the option to make any changes it deems necessary, and be willing to guarantee the re-design through performance guarantees. The point is that accountability must be defined and guarantees established. Risk management will not be successful if confusion exists as to who bears what risks.

In the Chandler, Arizona, privatization project, design of the treatment facility had begun before any privatization proposals were considered. Therefore, in the privatization service agreement, the design engineer who previously was retained by the community, was directly incorporated into the privatization project and was given a number of responsibilities. The engineer's role included:

- Finalizing design and participating in design reviews.
- Reaching concurrence on any design modifications proposed by the privatizer.
- Approving the division of construction contracts for competitive bidding and the final decisions for contract awards.
- Inspecting construction and carrying on other appropriate activities during the construction phase, outlined as "Basic Services" in the American Society of Civil Engineers Manual No. 45 (1975).
- Reviewing all change orders on behalf of the community.
- Consulting with the privatizer on the development of an operations and maintenance manual for the facility.

The community should also require that the privatizer have certain types of construction insurance, such as general liability and builder's insurance, that cover both the private firm and the community. Insurance, however, is no substitute for demonstrated experience. If the time required to put the facility in operation is especially important to the community, it may seek to impose a penalty on the private firm for late completion. Such was the case in the City of Orlando's request for privatization proposals.

Privatization of its wastewater treatment facility means that a community will be placing an essential service related to public health in the hands of a private firm. While the private firm will be under contractual obligation to meet certain performance requirements, the importance of selecting a qualified operator cannot be overstated. Firm credentials, as well as the credentials of the individuals to be involved in the local project should be carefully evaluated.

Communities should require performance guarantees from the private operator. These guarantees are likely to include monetary penalties for non-compliance and contract termination clauses for extended non-performance. The community may wish to require that the privatizer post a performance bond for successful execution of the contract, and additional pollution liability insurance to cover incidents associated with system malfunctions that could be detrimental to the environment. The private firm could also be asked to propose a methodology for controlling odors, lights and noise from the plant, and any other negative environmental impacts which may result from construction and operation of the facility. These measures reduce the community's risks and the private operator's risks as well. The private firm's cost of obtaining these bonds or implementing methodologies to control odors and noise will be shared with the community through the service charge. In addition to bonding and insurance, operating risks can be allocated in other ways.

To some extent, the private firm's risk of increased operating costs can be reduced by including cost escalation clauses in the contract for operation of the facility. While specific increases need not be agreed to in advance, the indices or formula to be used to calculate these increases can be established. This approach would be appropriate to handle the operating cost increases which occur due to increases in items such as power and chemicals. Other approaches would include structuring the operations and maintenance costs aspects of the project on a cost plus management fee basis. However, the community would have to be assured that the facility was being operated in a most cost-effective manner.

Under privatization, the private sector firm operating a facility has responsibilities in addition to those it would have if the municipality had constructed the facility and contracted for operation. Investors in the facility will be concerned about plant performance, and will hold the operator accountable for its performance. In addition, the state may be more likely to enforce fines and penalties on a private firm for non-compliance with discharge requirements, than take the more lenient attitude which is sometimes extended to municipalities.

Other operating risks should be handled on a site-specific basis. Some communities are more willing than others to share the responsibility for changes in regulations, legislation and options for disposal of treatment residuals.

In addition to operating guarantees, a community must be able to satisfy itself that the private firm is making the investments in repair and rehabilitation necessary to keep the plant operating properly. The community may want to conduct periodic inspections and receive fiscal and operational audits of the private firm's records relating to the facility.

Construction and operating risks can directly impact the economics of a privatization project. Chapter VI, Financing, includes a discussion of the specific effects on project economics of both construction and operating risks. However, in addition to construction and operating risks, there are specific financial risks.

FINANCIAL RISKS

The financial risks associated with a privatization transaction are risks which every private firm takes when it makes a capital-intensive investment and/or undertakes a new business venture. Once a privatization transaction is conceived, it can be structured to decrease financial risk. A sound financing and operating plan are integral to a privatization transaction. Credit enhancements which are discussed in Chapter VI and different types of operating insurance, such as business interruption insurance, should be considered for a privatization transaction. These items will provide greater security and protection for all parties involved. The additional costs, or portions thereof can be recovered through the service fee charged for the provision of treatment service, without materially affecting the significant economic savings afforded through the privatization concept. Financial risk can be viewed as a concern of the privatizer, but the public partner must be sensitive to the risks and understand what steps are being taken to ensure the financial integrity of the project. Given that communities may lack the internal expertise to evaluate financial risks to the privatizer, the community typically should have an independent financial advisor on its privatization selection and negotiation team.

RISKS SPECIFIC TO PRIVATIZATION

Risks specific to privatization are few, and if proper steps are taken, they can be eliminated. These risks, which are usually a function of an inadequate implementation plan, include:

- Misunderstanding of the privatization concept.
- Inadequate consideration of special interest groups.

• Delays in legislation allowing privatization to go forward.

The City of Orlando, Florida, asked specifically about risks when it issued a detailed Request for Proposals (RFP) to pre-qualified firms for the financing, construction, ownership, operation and maintenance of a 15 mgd advanced wastewater treatment facility. Specifically related to protecting its interests, the City requested that proposers identify the risks that the private firm proposed be assigned to the City. The City advised in the RFP that, to some extent, it was willing to absorb certain risks. The City indicated that it might accept responsibility for the quantity and quality of the wastewater flow delivered to the facility for treatment, and for changes in regulatory agency policies or procedures relating to discharge permits.

In structuring the privatization approach, a community may want to include provisions related to special interest groups, which would ease the acceptance and implementation of privatization. For example, a community may want to stipulate that public employees at an existing treatment facility be incorporated into the privatized plant's work force. Similarly, the community may desire that the selected privatizer give preference to local businesses as suppliers and vendors. Another example of consideration for special interest groups is related to Minority and Women-owned Business Enterprise (MBE and WBE) requirements. A community considering privatization may want to require that proposers commit themselves to comply with MBE and WBE requirements. Such was the case in the Orlando RFP.

The "expected" passage of privatization legislation may be viewed as a potential risk because legislative delays could affect potential project schedules. But actions taken by local governments to date indicate that the risk of legislative enactment is not a major one. In a number of the privatization projects already under way, communities have looked to the state government for laws to allow long-term contracting for sewage treatment services. Utah has already passed a privatization act (see Appendix B). In certain other states, on the basis of proposed legislation, a number of communities have begun the privatization process and issued Requests for Qualifications (RFQ) for privatization of their wastewater treatment facilities, or have actually commenced vendor negotiations.

It is interesting to note that the proposed New Jersey Wastewater Treatment Privatization Act (see Appendix C), makes specific mention that contracts for privatization must include mechanisms for the allocation of risks, including construction and financing cost overruns and operation and maintenance (O&M) risks. Communities in other states are recognizing these risks as well, and are asking the private sector to propose methods of allocating and managing them.

Without a clear understanding of privatization, a community will not be able to protect its interest adequately. While a city manager, public works director or other city official who is managing privatization implementation for a community needs an in-depth, detailed understanding of the concept, many others will need to have a general overview of privatization. Public education is essential. If the general public does not understand the concept and the oversight controls which are being placed on the private firm, they may feel that their economic well-being, health, or environmental conditions are in potential jeopardy. The community must understand that its elected leaders have certain key elements of oversight control with respect to the system.

These controls should be considered as safeguards, not reins. There is no substitute for having a trustworthy and responsible partner. The key to avoiding the selection of an inappropriate privatizer is for the community to establish a procurement process which pays due attention to qualifications and selection process criteria, a subject presented in greater detail in Chapter III.

Often, members of the community will express their concerns in more general terms, such as: "What happens if the facility is improperly operated?", or "What happens if it breaks down?"

The concerns should be appropriately addressed in the service agreement between the private firm and the community. A community may want the contract to require the private firm to pay a pre-determined fine if the facility fails to meet discharge requirements or if it becomes inoperational for reasons within the operator's control. Furthermore, the community may require the right to replace an operator if continuing operating problems occur which should have been avoidable. Part of the discussion in Chapter III centered on the different management systems and oversight programs that would allow the community to gauge the performance of a private operator. If such systems are put in place and properly monitored, concerns of performance may be more easily met.

In the privatization service contract, the community should obtain guarantees for items such as construction completion, treatment standards, operating and maintenance commitments, costs of service, provisions for facility purchase at the end of the contract period, etc. The private firm should get commitments from the community which include long-term service, influent quality, costs and payments for service. The reader is referred to Chapter VII, Legal Issues, for further discussion of the key aspects of privatization contracts.

SUMMARY

A community will face fewer risks by meeting its wastewater treatment needs through privatization, instead of through more conventional financing methods. In seeking a facility through privatization, the community will want assurances of quality design and construction, and of long-term, continuous operation during which the plant meets pre-determined performance standards. The community will want to achieve these goals at a cost lower than it could otherwise obtain. These objectives must be balanced against the needs of the private sector, which include a fair return on investment and assurances of a long-term business relationship that can enable the realization of economic benefits.

Compromise between the public and private sectors is an essential part of the privatization partnership. The time to compromise and establish mechanisms for the allocation of risk is during the contract negotiations. In many cases, the private sector can minimize risks through techniques such as bonding and insurance. The public sector must carry out its part of the responsibility by identifying risks and participating in the process of minimizing the risks. In practical terms, risk management and compromise means that some of the costs incurred to minimize risk will be passed on to the public sector through the service fee. However, the financial impact should be immaterial to a project's economics, whereas the comfort established should be significant.

VI FINANCING

*"Private financing of public works may become a trend in
the water pollution control business as Wall Street and
management-consultants help states and local governments
find sources to replace federal funds."*

Engineering News-Record
August 26, 1982

Conceiving a financing strategy and structuring the privatization transaction are among the most important aspects of privatization implementation. As discussed in Chapter III, there are many factors that must be considered in determining the feasibility of privatization, but if the numbers don't work, the project will never get off the ground. The type of financing strategy followed, and its cost, are key to making the numbers work.

In addition to financial feasibility based on anticipated costs and revenues, the transaction must be financeable. It must incorporate security and credit support elements that will be acceptable to both debt and equity investors, and must be competitively attractive when compared to other investment opportunities that are available in the debt and equity markets.

Privatization is unlike traditional public finance approaches, because it incorporates both debt and equity capital. Another difference is that

67

privatization offers an opportunity for a community and the private sector to work together to use alternative financing concepts, such as industrial development bonds (IDBs), to fund the bulk of the project cost, rather than using municipal debt-based vehicles.

Communities have, in the past, typically used general obligation (GO) bonds to finance water and sewer improvements. GO issues are considered part of a community's outstanding indebtedness, and therefore, considered in the calculation of the statutory debt ceilings imposed by certain state governments, and in covenants on existing debt. By using industrial development bonds, pollution control revenue bonds, the commercial credit of the private sector or other revenue-based "project financing" techniques, which are not included in computing community debt, privatization enables local governments to use their limited debt capacity for other essential purposes.

Although new to wastewater treatment financing, privatization of traditionally "public" activities is not a new concept to either the debt or equity markets. Several major resource recovery projects have been structured as privatization transactions, using combinations of tax-exempt and taxable debt (IDBs) and equity. Because privatization principles have been accepted in this and other fields, the investment community is supportive of privatization, perhaps even more so than of traditional funding methods used in the wastewater treatment industry. Privatization offers advantages over conventional revenue bond funding, which is now becoming prevalent in water and sewage facility financings. If properly structured, privatization may have more appeal to the investment community. Reasons for this attractiveness include:

- Inherent in privatization are contractual commitments for operating and maintenance standards, which, in effect, assure that physical plant assets will be maintained. In fact, such strong assurances are not usually found in traditionally "public" projects. These assurances preserve the value of the investors' holdings. If a facility is purchased from the investors at some time in the future, the selling price is likely to reflect the fair market value of a well maintained and operable asset.

- The investment community will work more closely with the private sector, establishing valuable relationships on which to base similar and other types of financial services in the future.

Before considerations of transaction structuring and security are made, the need for the project must be established. The cost savings possible with privatization cannot be substituted as a development incentive for a real need for a project. By being comfortable with the assessment of a project's need, potential debt and equity investors will have confidence that, in the event of technical or financial problems, all parties involved will work together to find remedies and keep the project operating, and, therefore, generating revenues. This presumption can be supported as long as it can be documented that users are dependent on continued plant performance for the maintenance of public health. The current and projected economic health of the service area is also key to developing investor confidence.

STRUCTURING THE PRIVATIZATION TRANSACTION

Appropriately structuring a privatization transaction requires expertise in the areas of public and project financing, industry specific conventions, tax and other areas. (1) A private sector firm interested in pursuing privatization opportunities must avail itself of the necessary advisors. A community interested in evaluating privatization approaches needs to select a qualified financial advisor who can competently compare the economics of privatization to alternative financing approaches and review the financing transaction structured by the private sector and its advisors. The community must assure itself that the financing plan does not put the community or the project at unneccessary risk and that it is structured to achieve the maximum economic benefits.

In wastewater privatization financings, the challenge is to structure the transaction so that both components, debt and equity, are competitive with other market offerings. For the equity, considerations of return and risk will be paramount. For the debt, whether tax-exempt or taxable, marketability will be determined by the rating given to the bonds, as well as to the structure of the issue and its appeal to retail and institutional buyers. Weakness in either component will jeopardize the transaction's ability to be financed. In addition to marketability, the structuring process must address the effect of the transaction on the financial position of the privatizer, and the security for the transaction (security elements are discussed in a later section of this chapter).

Although it is theoretically possible, and perhaps practical on smaller projects, for an owner to provide equity to finance the entire facility cost, it is usually advantageous to finance the majority or all of the cost through the issuance of debt, normally accomplished through the sale of tax-exempt bonds. Absent any limitations due to the application of "at risk" tax rules (see Appendix A), an investor in a wastewater treatment facility will be entitled to tax benefits calculated on the full cost of the facility, even if the equity invested, if any, is only a small percentage of the full project cost. Most potential investors prefer to "leverage" their investments through a number of debt/equity deals, rather than investing all of their available equity in one project to finance it without debt.

The use of debt to finance most or all of a project's capital costs raises the issue of how the incurrence of that debt will impact the privatizer. Many potential privatizers are publicly-held companies which are concerned about the annual reporting of their financial results and conditions to shareholders and the financial community. As a result, many will seek to structure privatization transactions in a manner which utilizes "off-balance sheet, non-recourse" techniques. The most common of these techniques is "project financing."

In its purest form, project financing is a method of borrowing funds for a project in which the lender's security for the loan is based on the expectation that revenues generated by the project will be sufficient to service the debt incurred for the project; the lender, typically, also will demand a mortgage on the assets of the project entity. In addition, the privatizer may have to provide an equity investment and certain other guarantees, such as a cash deficiency agreement, debt service reserve fund, letter of credit, etc. Such items are blended into the financing transaction.

Under traditional methods of raising funds, the borrower raises money on the basis of his own direct credit and not on the basis of project revenues. Lenders look to the overall creditworthiness of the borrower and all of the borrower's assets as security for their loan, not only to the assets and revenue from a single project. In project financing, lenders do not have direct recourse to the privatizer's assets or revenue, but rely on the economics of the project, project-specific security provisions, contractor and service recipient guarantees, project assets and the revenue stream generated by the project, for their security.

Chandler, Arizona perceived security-related differences between the two approaches. The City gave proposers the option of proposing with or without equity investment. The City did not require equity investment if the security for the transaction was, in essence, the credit of the proposer (i.e., on-balance sheet). A minimum equity investment of 20% was required of proposers who proposed to secure the transaction through project revenues and other project-based aspects (i.e., off-balance sheet). The equity investment was to act as an incentive for performance, as well as a device to reduce costs. At closing, the Chandler transaction included no equity contribution. To have Chandler accept 100% debt financing, the private firm "guaranteed" the debt with its own credit and also provided a back-up guarantee in the form of a letter of credit from a major bank.

Properly structured project financing arrangements will, among other things:

- Preserve the borrowing capacity and the creditworthiness of the privatizer;

- May avoid recording a liability for the debt portion of the project on the sponsor's balance sheet; this may be important to avoid indenture restrictions on issuing additional debt, and otherwise avoid impairment of the sponsor's balance sheet.

Given the fact that many of the private sector groups active in privatization include publicly-held corporations or companies with existing outstanding debt and related debt covenants, it can be reasonably expected that the "off-balance sheet, non-recourse" mode of structuring projects will become common, especially since some form of debt instrument can be expected to provide the bulk of the financing for most privatization projects.

Determining the appropriate debt/equity mix, and the timing of the equity investment, are crucial elements in the structuring of the transaction. An approach in which the equity contribution is carefully planned will improve the economics of the transaction. For example, a portion of the equity can be provided at the beginning of a project, with subsequent contributions made according to a pre-determined schedule during construction and/or operation to meet specified cash needs of the project.

Municipalities must recognize that they will be somewhat limited in dictating equity investment terms and conditions, the amount of equity invested and the return expected. The municipality must accommodate the demands of the equity market, or it will not be able to attract the equity required.

OWNERSHIP ALTERNATIVES

The economic benefits of privatization are dependent upon the approach taken by the municipality and the private firm, as discussed in Chapter II, and on the financing and ownership structure utilized. The three most common structures for privatization financing are 100% vendor ownership, limited partnership and leveraged lease. As more transactions are conceived and completed, more approaches will be developed.

100% Vendor Ownership: In 100% ownership by a single vendor, ownership is by a single tax-paying entity. Typically, the vendor is involved in the construction and/or operation of the facility. The structure is illustrated in Figure VI-1. By assuming ownership of the facility, the private sector firm qualifies for tax benefits. (2) With 100% vendor ownership, an actual equity investment may not be necessary, as the project could be financed entirely with debt.

Typically, in the single vendor ownership transaction, the owner contributes an equity portion after the completion of construction. The vendor/owner enters into a service contract with the community for the provision of wastewater treatment services. The community makes service payments in return for receiving the service. The vendor is responsible for making the debt service payments on the bonds and receives the tax benefits related to the project. This approach will most likely be used for relatively smaller projects because a single owner will be limited in his ability to be responsible for the debt on many projects. Frequently, a corporation will form a special purpose subsidiary as the actual owner/operator of the project and, then, guarantee the performance of that subsidiary.

The principal advantage of the single owner transaction is that it is less complex than other approaches, and consequently easier and quicker to implement. The principal drawback is that, even if the security for the transaction is project-based, the financing or the guarantees provided may have to be reflected on the owner's (or parent corporation's) balance sheet. The field of companies that are financially able or willing to assume such a liability is narrow.

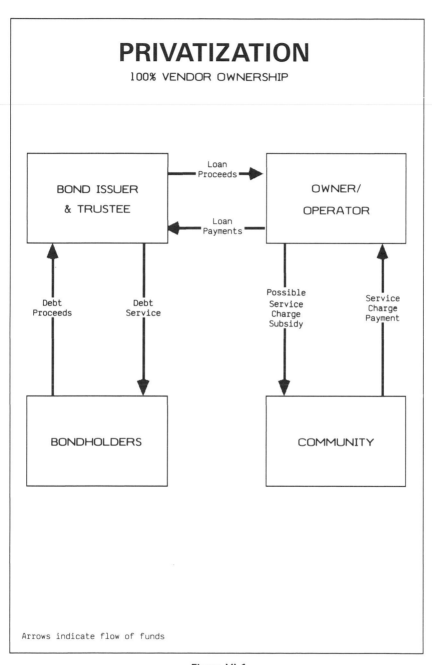

Figure VI-1

Limited Partnership: A limited partnership structure is shown in Figure VI-2. This approach can be used when a private sector firm wants to privatize a project but does not have a large enough tax liability to use all the tax benefits. The firm can form a partnership to share ownership, and therefore share the business opportunity, risks and benefits.

If a limited partnership approach is used, the facility is financed through a combination of equity, provided by the partnership, and debt. As in the 100% ownership approach, the partnership is able to claim tax benefits based on the full cost of the facility, while only providing equity equal to a portion of the costs. Partnership tax treatment allows the gains and losses on the project to be passed through to the partners, rather than remaining in the entity, as in corporations. Project returns are split among the partners in relative proportion to their investments or other agreed upon arrangements. The limited partners typically are parties seeking tax benefits and cash returns.

Typically, there are two types of owners in a limited partnership, a general partner and a group of passive limited partners. The general partner has unlimited liability and is responsible for the organization and management of the partnership. Therefore, the general partner or an affiliate is usually entitled, in addition to his project returns, to an annual management fee and, in some cases, an organization fee. The limited partners typically are limited in their liability to the amount invested or to an amount specified in the partnership agreement. The limited partners are also limited in their day-to-day control over the project.

The limited partnership structure is attractive for a number of reasons. For example, a construction or engineering firm which is interested in privatizing a facility will typically act as the general partner. In this capacity, the firm will deal directly on a day-to-day basis with the community, and will most likely have operating responsibility. The difference between this structure and 100% vendor ownership is that the private firm, with the help of its financial advisors, syndicates a portion of the ownership to a group of passive investors. Acquiring only partial ownership in a facility may allow the investors a more favorable balance sheet treatment of the transaction. The limited partnership structure is beneficial to the transaction since it spreads the ownership of the facility to investors who can adequately assume the benefits and risks of ownership, while still maintaining the general partner as a direct link between the community and the private sector partnership. Since the general part-

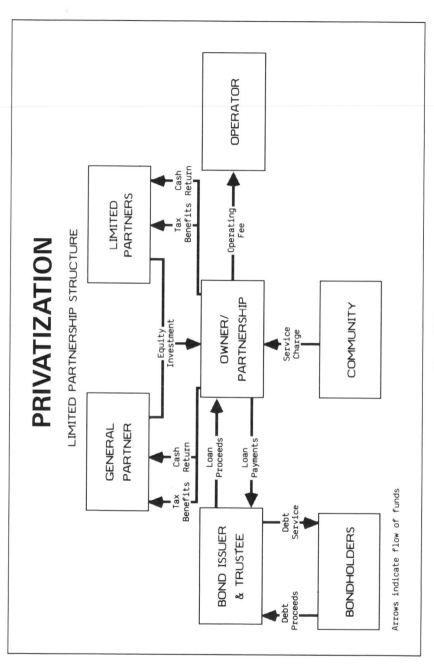

PRIVATIZATION

LIMITED PARTNERSHIP STRUCTURE

Arrows indicate flow of funds

Figure VI-2

ner usually acts as the operator (and, perhaps, designer/builder), passive partners need to be confident of the technical and financial capabilities of the general partner in order to be attracted to the investment initially. Without a strong, capable builder/operator, equity investment cannot be attracted.

Special considerations of this approach include:

- The equity investment can significantly reduce the debt financing requirements and, as a result, the service contract fees;
- Limited partners are passive investors, and are precluded from participating in the operation of the facility;
- The field of potential investors and, therefore, sources of equity, is broader than under 100% ownership. However, it may be difficult to attract investors if substantial cash contributions are required over a lengthy period;
- A relatively high internal rate of return on invested equity capital is currently required to market limited partnerships;
- The time horizon of most prospective investors is usually shorter than the project life. This may require structuring an agreement in which the original owners of the facility have the right, subject to municipal approval, to sell the facility to other investors before the bonds are retired or before the municipality may choose to exercise a purchase option;
- The transaction is complex, time-consuming and more expensive to structure;
- The amount of equity to be invested will be conditioned by project needs, as well as investor requirements and the attractiveness of competing investments in the market; the resolution of these issues will require substantive negotiations.

Leveraged Lease: In the leveraged lease structure, presented in Figure VI-3, the equity investment is provided by a passive, third-party investor such as a bank, leasing company or other financial institution. The financial institution (the lessor) purchases the privatized facility through a combination of equity and debt. This structure is called a "leveraged" lease because debt capital makes up approximately 60% to 80% of the facility cost. The lessor takes the tax benefits of ownership and leases

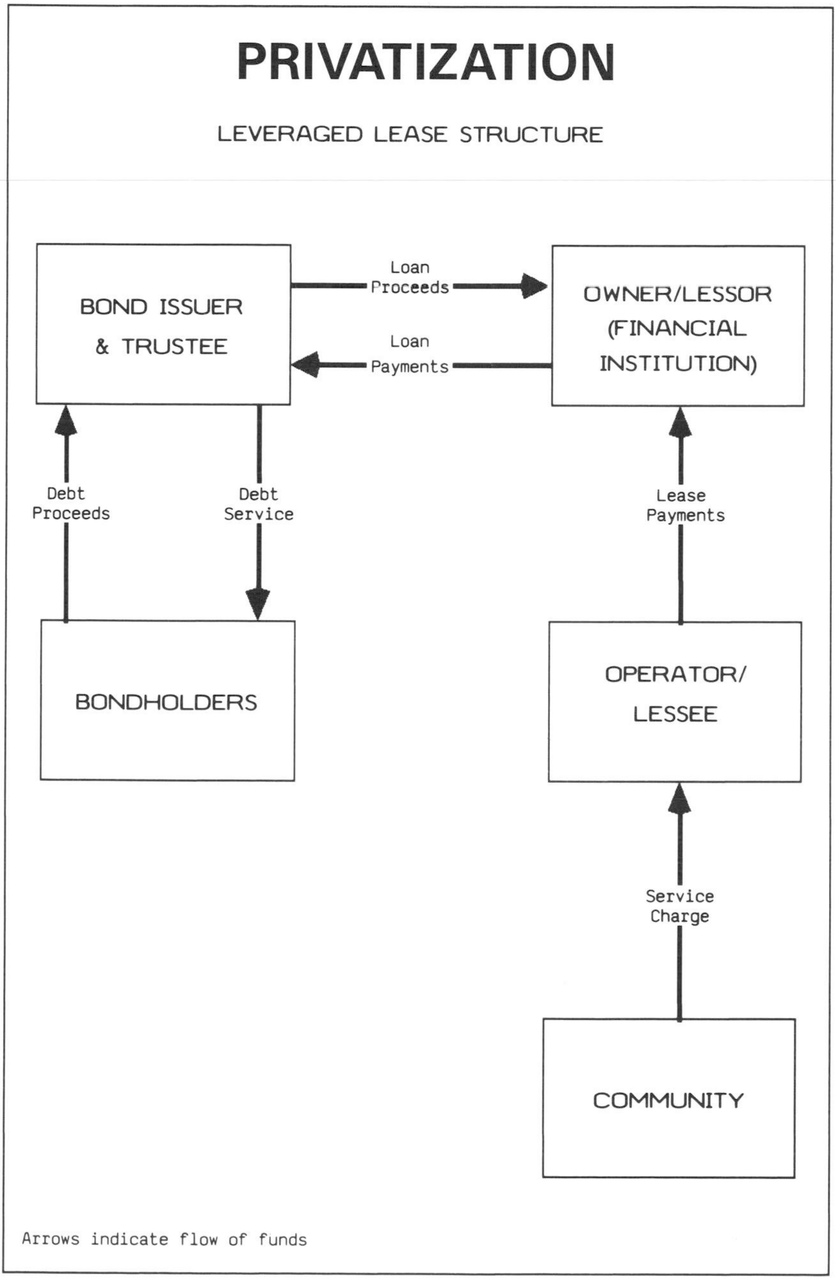

PRIVATIZATION

LEVERAGED LEASE STRUCTURE

```
┌─────────────────┐      Loan          ┌─────────────────┐
│                 │    Proceeds ──────▶│  OWNER/LESSOR   │
│  BOND ISSUER    │─────────────       │  (FINANCIAL     │
│  & TRUSTEE      │      Loan           │  INSTITUTION)   │
│                 │◀── Payments ───────│                 │
└─────────────────┘                    └─────────────────┘
   ▲        │                                    ▲
   │        │                                    │
  Debt     Debt                                Lease
 Proceeds  Service                            Payments
   │        │                                    │
   │        ▼                                    │
┌─────────────────┐                    ┌─────────────────┐
│                 │                    │                 │
│  BONDHOLDERS    │                    │   OPERATOR/     │
│                 │                    │    LESSEE       │
│                 │                    │                 │
└─────────────────┘                    └─────────────────┘
                                                ▲
                                                │
                                             Service
                                              Charge
                                                │
                                       ┌─────────────────┐
                                       │                 │
                                       │   COMMUNITY     │
                                       │                 │
                                       │                 │
                                       └─────────────────┘
```

Arrows indicate flow of funds

Figure VI-3

the facility to another private sector firm, the lessee. The lessee is the actual user of the facility and is the firm with the day-to-day operational responsibility and the direct contact with the community. In return for the use of the facility, the lessee makes lease payments to the owner, who in turn, makes payments on the debt. The leveraged lease structure is a lease between two private sector firms, the owner and the operator. The operator enters into a service contract with the municipality and receives service payments for provision of the wastewater treatment service.

Special considerations of this approach include:

- The after-tax internal rate of return required by the leveraged lease investor is typically somewhat lower than that of the limited partner, due to the different financial needs of the investing financial institutions. This may increase the amount of equity which can be sold and reduce the amount of debt financing required, reducing the required service fee;

- Properly structured, the lease obligation between the lessor and lessee will be an operating lease under Financial Accounting Standards Board (FASB) 13 (as opposed to a capital lease) and, therefore, will not have to be capitalized on the lessee's balance sheet;

- Assuming identical service fees, the total return to the lessee may be greater under this approach than to a general partner under a partnership structure;

- The lessor is much more risk averse than the limited partner and will require the municipality and the lessee, or other parties, to bear a greater share of the risk;

- The lessee's exposure includes deficiencies in service contract payments by the municipality; consequently, the lessee must be comfortable with the credit of the community and the community's willingness and ability to collect user fees or otherwise make service payments;

- The field of potential leveraged lease investors may be narrower than that for limited partners transactions.

The lease equity market is well established for equipment and is becoming increasingly popular for capital-intensive facilities. Like the partnership approach, it can be a particularly valuable form of transaction structure in the situation where the privatizing firm cannot make the most efficient use of all available tax benefits. Construction or engineering firms which are interested in privatization often have cyclical income patterns and therefore cannot accurately predict their income tax liability. On the other hand, a leasing company or other financial institution is in the business of making this type of investment, and can predict its tax liabilities with more precision. Leveraged leasing transactions can be complicated, and are best suited to large projects where the returns are sufficient to justify the increased transaction costs.

Both the leveraged lease and the limited partnership structure require specific contracts and agreements. A discussion of privatization documentation is included in Chapter VII.

INDUSTRIAL DEVELOPMENT BONDS: AN ADDED PLUS

In privatization transactions, it is possible for the private sector to provide equity capital at amounts equal to twenty-five percent or less of the total project cost, and to have the remainder of the cost financed by tax-exempt industrial development bonds (IDBs). In some specific cases, even higher percentages of debt financing may be possible. However, the mix of debt and equity for each transaction should be evaluated on a project-specific basis.

IDBs are issued by a city, county or state authority on behalf of the private sector. In order to issue IDBs, the particular government unit must be specifically authorized by state law to issue tax-exempt debt for use by private entities. Typically, water and sewer authorities and similar utility agencies are not empowered to loan bond proceeds to private parties. Therefore, industrial development or pollution control authorities are the usual issuers. Who issues the bond may affect the cost of issuance. A number of states charge placement fees for issuing bonds. If the bonds are sold to the public, a trustee will usually be appointed to act under the terms of an indenture, which sets out the financial duties and obligations of the borrower.

IDBs are not, under any circumstances, a general obligation of the governmental entity which issues them. In the case of a privatization approach, which incorporates a service agreement between the community and a private sector firm, the bonds are typically secured by a "take-or-pay" or "take-and-pay" provision in the agreement (3), along with conventional elements such as debt service reserve funds, rate covenants and, perhaps, some form of credit enhancement. This is an example of project financing, where bondholders look to the project itself for security, rather than to the credit of the community or the privatizer. A typical privatization transaction using IDB financing is diagramed in Figure VI-4.

Transactions need not be financed with IDBs. Traditional forms of debt can be used to finance privatization projects. However, in most cases, IDBs, because of their lower cost tax-exempt interest, provide the lowest cost debt source that can be used while still retaining the ability to utilize tax benefits. Tax-exempt IDBs can sell with interest rates of approximately 70% or less of long-term, taxable issues. Tax exemption creates a strong market for well-secured bonds.

A condition for the interest to be considered tax-exempt income to the bondholders is that substantially all of the proceeds of the bond issue are to be used to provide the exempt facility. This is known as the "substantially all" test. According to tax code regulations, "substantially all" is generally considered to be 90% of the proceeds of the issue. The proceeds of the bond issue are reduced by any amount which, on a pro rata basis, is allocable between providing the exempt facility and other uses of the proceeds. (4)

EFFECT OF THE NEW TAX LAWS

The "cap" on the issuance of tax-exempt IDBs contained in the Deficit Reduction Act of 1984 limits the amount of IDB funds that can be available in any state during any one year. Privatization sponsors will be in competition with traditional IDB users for these limited allocations, both at the local and state levels. The obvious "public purpose" nature of privatization strongly argues for priority being given to wastewater treatment projects in state and local IDB allocations under the cap.

Privatization sponsors, however, should acknowledge the possibility that they will not be included in the annual allocation process. Therefore, as part of an overall privatization feasibility analysis, they should assess alternatives to tax-exempt financing. The more practicable options include:

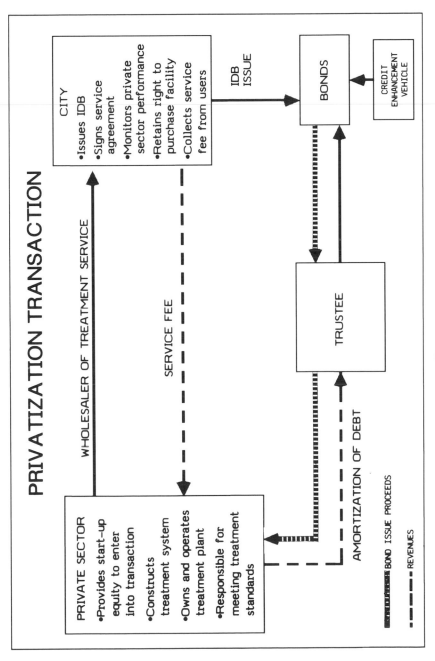

PRIVATIZATION TRANSACTION

CITY
- Issues IDB
- Signs service agreement
- Monitors private sector performance
- Retains right to purchase facility
- Collects service fee from users

IDB ISSUE

BONDS

CREDIT ENHANCEMENT VEHICLE

WHOLESALER OF TREATMENT SERVICE

SERVICE FEE

TRUSTEE

AMORTIZATION OF DEBT

PRIVATE SECTOR
- Provides start-up equity to enter into transaction
- Constructs treatment system
- Owns and operates treatment plant
- Responsible for meeting treatment standards

BOND ISSUE PROCEEDS

REVENUES

Figure VI-4

Commercial loans: Bank loans may be appropriate for smaller projects, those that offer shorter-term paybacks (7-10 years), those that are not overly sensitive to interest rates, and those that include particularly strong owner financial guarantees. Given the "infrastructure" nature of wastewater treatment and the expected long-term use and service life of facilities, longer-term loans may be available. Privatization loans may be attractive to a major bank (or a consortium of banks) located in a project's service area.

Taxable IDBs: Taxable bonds will carry a higher interest rate than tax-exempt issues and may have higher debt service coverage ratio requirements. However, they frequently do not carry the same reserve fund requirements, which can reduce the amount of debt initially issued. Taxable debt can be sold at public sale (requiring Securities Exchange Commission registration) or by private placement. The market for floating rate taxable debt is not as well developed as that for tax-exempt debt. Because taxable bonds are in competition with the bonds and other paper of banks, banks are reluctant to "compete with themselves" by issuing letters of credit for taxable bonds.

Tax-exempt/Taxable combinations: A resource recovery plant in North Andover, Massachusetts was financed with a simultaneously issued combination of tax-exempt and taxable bonds. Although issued separately, the two types of debt can be secured under the same indenture on a parity basis, with no subordination of either, and with the flow of funds managed by a single trustee. Such a combination may be attractive to sponsors who receive allocations of tax-exempt IDBs adequate to finance a portion, but not all, of their projects. The lower interest cost of the tax-exempt bonds will mitigate the effects of the taxable bond's higher rate.

Equipment Leasing: The capital needs of a project and the amount of debt required can be reduced by leasing certain pieces of equipment directly from vendors, rather than purchasing the equipment. Lease payments would be reflected in annual O&M costs, rather than in annual debt service. This approach may be attractive for projects with inadequate tax-exempt IDB allocations or for those using more costly taxable debt.

Vendor Creativity: In the absence of other alternatives, sponsoring communities can turn to their prospective contractors for financing ideas. Contractors may have relations with venture capital groups, commercial banks and financing institutions, or other financing sources. Although the cost for such financing may be higher than other approaches, the mutual understanding between the community and the contractor that the approach is the only option should create a positive climate for negotiations.

Choosing a transaction structure and financing vehicle which will provide the greatest economic benefits to the private sector has advantages for the public sector as well. The lower the project costs to the private sector, the lower will be the service charge asked of the community. This means that the user fees which will be charged by the local government unit to individual users of the system will be lower as well.

DEBT FINANCING REQUIREMENTS

Our discussion of debt financing requirements relates specifically to tax-exempt bonds. Although sponsors may face difficulty in certain states in receiving adequate IDB allocations under the new tax law, IDBs should be pursued whenever possible because they usually represent the lowest cost debt financing available. Every effort should be made to assure that privatization projects receive allocation priority. The tax law provides some preferential treatment in terms of states' abilities to carry forward unused, annual IDB allotments for pollution control facilities.

While this discussion is keyed to the tax-exempt market, an emphasis on security will be found in either the tax-exempt or taxable debt market. Lenders are not speculators. Although specific security measures may vary between different types of transactions, the degree of security required by lenders will not vary significantly. Many of the specific elements, including wastewater delivery and service payment guarantees, procedures to adjust fees, strong and enforceable contract cost and performance guarantees and comprehensive insurance coverage will be demanded by any type of lender. Just as potential equity investors assess prospective risks and returns, potential bond buyers perform a similar assessment of a debt issue. Regardless of the type of ownership and equity investment, privatization projects have one common element; most rely on debt for a substantial portion of the financing and they must respond to the demands of the debt market.

When potential bond buyers consider investments, they look to the bond rating given by Standard and Poor's Corporation (S&P) or Moody's Investor Services, the two principal rating agencies. The rating indicates the amount of risk involved, and as a result, helps determine the interest rate on the issue. For example, an S&P rating of "AAA" means that there is an "extremely strong" capacity to pay principal and interest; an "A" rating means there is a "strong capacity". If an "AAA" issue carried an interest rate of 10%, an "A" rated issue may have a 10.25 to 10.5% interest rate. A bond investor will accept a lower rate of return than an equity investor in exchange for a greater likelihood of a return: "bond buyers aren't risk takers" is one of the oldest investment banking adages.

In structuring the debt portion of the transaction, the target should be a security structure which will earn at least an "A" rating. Significant interest penalties (higher rates) will be paid for lower or non-rated issues. While project-specific circumstances will determine the security structure of each privatization financing, the types of elements that rating agencies and investors will look for will include:

- A feasibility study performed to document the technical and financial feasibility of the project, and the current and projected economic ability of the service area to support the project under a variety of scenarios;

- A firm commitment for any equity required, secured by instruments such as irrevocable letters of credit, if equity is to be invested in any manner other than fully at the time of bond closing;

- A debt service reserve fund equal to one year's principal and interest, and possibly other reserve funds for operation and maintenance costs and equipment repair and replacement needs;

- A municipal guarantee of the life-of-the-bonds availability of specified volumes of wastewater to the project, along with a covenant by the municipality not to allow competing projects;

- Collection of individual user fees by the municipality, under a rate covenant of the municipality to levy and collect whatever rates are required to fulfill municipal financial obligations to the project;

- Procedures to adjust service charges to reflect increased costs due to conditions such as inflation, force majeure, changes in legislation, etc.;

- Strong construction, operating cost and long-term performance guarantees by principal contractors (such as the builder and/or builder/operator) which are enforceable because of contractors' (or parent corporation's) financial and technical capabilities.

PARTICIPANTS

The implementation of a privatization project involves more diverse financial disciplines than are found in the typical water or wastewater treatment financing.

For any debt financing, the managing underwriter (investment banker) will, as the underwriter and marketer of the debt, have the final authority for all principal security and structuring aspects of the transaction. It will be the manager's responsibility to determine, in accordance with the owner's and the community's goals and objectives, the type of bonds to be used (i.e., terms vs. serials, zero coupon bonds, etc.), and other structural aspects, such as call and redemption conditions, based on project needs and prevailing market conditions and requirements. The underwriter will structure the issue to achieve the highest rating possible and to be competitive with the myriad of issues in the market at that time. The underwriter also will be responsible for the marketing of the bonds. The underwriter will have to make some "fine tuning" decisions related to bond size, structure, interest rate and other aspects of the bond issue immediately before the actual bond sale. For example, while the feasibility study may reflect an interest rate of 10.25%, actual market conditions at the time of sale may call for a 10.5% rate. The project must be sufficiently flexible to accommodate such last minute adjustments.

If equity investment is a part of the transaction, the underwriter may also structure and act as the equity syndicator for limited partnership shares or, in the case of leveraged leases, may negotiate with the owner/lessor.

The community will require the services of a financial advisor. It may be possible for one firm to act as both financial advisor and underwriter. However, special rules of the Municipal Securities Rulemaking Board apply in these cases, and, in general, questions of independence and objectivity are involved. Potential conflicts arise in this type of situation and "it is generally not in the jurisdiction's best interest to enter into a financial advisory relationship with a firm knowing that it intends to underwrite the bond issue."(5) Financial advisors assist and represent the municipality in the structuring of the project, both financial and contract elements, in contract negotiations, and, in general, in the community's relations with all other parties. The advisor can to a large degree serve as "staff" to the municipality by providing expertise which may not be available in the municipality, and as the "project co-manager" or coordinator of the privatization implementation program.

If IDB financing is used, a bond counsel will also be involved. Among the services provided by bond counsel are:

- Preparation and/or review of documents regarding sale and issuance of the bonds, including credit agreements or similar documents.

- Review of service, operations and construction contracts.

- Preparation of the financing agreement between the private sector and the issuer, and of the trust indenture.

- Rendering a final opinion on the validity and tax-exempt status of interest on the bonds.

IMPROVING THE TRANSACTION: CREDIT ENHANCEMENTS AND RISK REDUCTION

Once the privatization financing structure has been conceived, there may be ways in which it can be improved. One way is to improve the credit of the debt issue and another is to remove much of the risk associated with the construction and operation of the facility.

Credit enhancement mechanisms are not substitutes for the ability to repay debt, but are used to enhance credit ratings, lower interest costs and expand an issuer's access to the market. One type of credit enhancement applicable to tax-exempt issues is bond insurance. A borrower would obtain bond insurance prior to marketing the bonds. For a one-time premium of approximately 1.0% to 1.5% of the total principal and interest due on the insured bonds, the insurance guarantees timely payment of debt service. Once issued, a policy cannot be revoked, and will cover the full term of all bonds insured. In evaluating the benefits of bond insurance, a borrower must determine if the interest cost savings exceed the cost of the premium. Several firms provide bond insurance, but the American Municipal Bond Assurance Corporation (AMBAC), Municipal Bond Insurance Association (MBIA) and FGIC Corporation are the most well known.

Another way in which a project can guarantee payment of principal and interest is with a letter of credit (LC). By using a letter of credit the borrower is able to supplement his own credit with that of a bank, enabling the issue to obtain a stronger rating and, therefore, a lower interest rate on the debt. It must be determined if the interest savings are greater than the cost of the letter of credit, which is usually an annual fee of approximately 3/4% to 1 1/4% of the amount of the bonds outstanding. LCs typically are issued for less than 10 years but are usually renewable at the option of the bank or insurance company giving the LC. LCs are not as available for taxable debt issues as they are for tax-exempt issues. The 25-year tax-exempt initial issue of industrial development bonds for Chandler, Arizona's 5 mgd wastewater treatment plant was backed by a letter of credit.

Other types of credit enhancements exist, but the choice of which to use is dependent on the vehicle used to finance the project. For example, short-term bonds, such as variable rate notes and commercial paper may be backed by revolving credit agreements. Commercial paper can be used during construction to allow the issuer more time to select a long-term financing market. Variable rate notes, backed by LCs, usually provide initially lower interest costs because the interest rate fluctuates periodically with a prescribed municipal bond market index or an index based on a bank's prime lending rate. In a revolving credit agreement, a bank makes a loan to the issuer, who uses the loan to make interest and principal payments on the debt. Revolving credit is not an agreement to pay the bondholders. Therefore, the rating of an issue backed by revolving credit is based on the issuer's credit, not the bank's.

Credit enhancement mechanisms are not substitutes for inherently strong transactions; they cannot be used to bolster otherwise weak financings. If the fundamental elements of a project are not strong on their own, insurers or banks will not be amenable to giving credit enhancements.

CONSTRUCTION AND OPERATING RISKS

A transaction may also be improved by removing as many of the project risks as possible. Some risks will inevitably remain and these must be allocated among the parties, i.e., owners, contractors, operators, bondholders, users, etc., and then mitigated through concepts such as guarantees, support agreements and various types of insurance coverages. Chapter V identifies and discusses a number of privatization risks. However, two types of risk have a greater bearing on financing: construction and operating risks.

During the construction phase, the goal is to construct, on time and within budget, a facility which is capable of processing the waste loadings to a desired treatment level. If, for any reason, the construction is not completed within budget, runs into unanticipated delays or is never completed, the envisioned revenues from the service agreement will be diminished. Any perceived construction-related risks to continuous revenue flows will jeopardize the transaction's ability to be financed.

Project developers, typically, will be the major source of credit support for completion of the project. Although some may be reluctant to do so, developers may have to be prepared to guarantee the completion of the project within a specified time period at a "fixed or not-to-exceed price." Even the most creditworthy sponsors may be asked by the investment community to supplement their own guarantees with more formal types of credit enhancements, such as letters of credit or insurance. In the case of project financing on a non-recourse basis, i.e., limiting the liability of construction risk to the project sponsor, the following arrangements typically will be necessary to provide a substitute for the completion guarantee by the sponsor:

- A strong construction contract which
  1. is turnkey, i.e., requiring a certain standard of project performance;
  2. is "a fixed price" and guarantee, even if mechanisms for unanticipated but agreed to changes are included; and
  3. requires the contractor to bear responsibility for financing costs associated with delays and non-delivery by a certain date for non-force majeure delays.
- Extensive insurance which will pay the financing costs associated with force majeure delays and force majeure caused non-comple-

tion by a certain date, including the full repayment of the construction loan.

- Depending upon the financial condition of the contractors, a performance bond with respect to the obligations of the contractor under the construction agreement.
- Insurance which will repay the construction lender in the event of physical loss, damage or destruction of the project or physical components thereof.
- Commitments for permanent financing for the project, including acceptable provisions for cost overruns, delays, etc., which are acceptable to construction period lenders.

Non-recourse financing during the construction of a project will, by definition, relieve the developer of the construction risks associated with the project. However, such financing will prove more expensive and will require significantly more time to complete. The developer may wish to consider providing a project completion guarantee which is included in the capitalized costs of the project.

In financing a project, consideration must also be given to issues which emerge after the treatment system is tested and successfully placed into service. Operating risks include the system's failure to provide an expected level of treatment, resulting in service charges and resultant profits that are insufficient to meet debt service obligations and provide the expected returns to equity holders. From a potential investor's perspective, such conditions could arise for a variety of reasons, including faulty design, inadequately-trained operators, unanticipated waste loadings entering the plant, disruptions to the supply of waste loadings, changes in environmental regulations, facility destruction by malicious intent or force majeure events, and inadequate spending for preventive maintenance.

To mitigate some of the operating risks, the local governing unit will have to commit to pay for treatment service as it is provided. The municipality will be expected to assume risks for some aspects, such as force majeure or changes in law which affect operation and maintenance costs. However, it is clearly inadvisable for the public sector to guarantee payment under any and all circumstances. One possible answer is to have business interruption or other form of insurance, performance guarantees by the creditworthy engineering, design and construction firms which design, build and operate the facility and guarantees by the equipment manufacturers regarding the performance of equipment. Such guarantees might obligate the groups involved to assume the responsibility for system or equipment performance for a predefined period of time, including the reponsibility for revenues lost as a result of non-performance.

These risk reduction measures necessarily add to project cost, but they can be funded in project capitalization or annual operating budgets, without substantially decreasing the expected savings available through privatization. More importantly, reduced risks provide further comfort that a facility will be established and properly operated and maintained to serve its basic function of effective treatment on a long-term basis.

As revenue-based projects, financing (either equity or debt) will be problematic without the assurance of on-time start-up and of specified performance. The importance of the role that construction and operations contractors play is obvious. But equally important, and perhaps from a financing perspective more important, is their financial capability to assume risk for their non-performance. These risks include absorbing non-accepted construction cost overruns, paying damages for late delivery and "buying down" both debt and equity for complete non-performance. Because late delivery may cause delays in the revenue stream to the project, damages could be tied to the debt service payments that the private firm will still be required to make in a timely fashion. The contractor may also be required to absorb losses of operation and maintenance cost overruns and mismanagement, and the cost of fines or penalties to regulatory bodies for violation of health and environmental standards. More important than the extent of any guarantees extracted is the enforceability of those guarantees. "Strong" guarantees provided by financially weak contractors are meaningless, and will imperil the financing as well as the project's ability to provide long-term service to the municipality and its residents.

INDUSTRY SPECIFIC FINANCING TOOLS

One very challenging aspect of privatization is to successfully blend project financing with environmental industry conventions to achieve the lowest possible "politically acceptable" user fees. Industry specific financial arrangements (i.e., connection fees, surcharges for high strength discharges, etc.) should be blended with the potential construction cost savings, tax advantages and tax-exempt financing vehicles of privatization. The benefits that result include lower user fees, more attractive cash flow sources for both the private and public sectors, and the ultimate transfer of ownership, if desired, to the public sector.

In conceiving the financing of a privatization transaction, some thought should be given to means of enabling the governmental unit to generate revenues to subsidize or stabilize user fees. These additional funds could also be used to finance the eventual purchase of the facility by the municipality. Two representative types of fees are discussed below. However, the appropriate fees and fee structures are dependent on many site-specific issues. These issues should be considered, and their impact evaluated before additional fees are imposed on the community.

Impact fees are a way of making growth pay its way by forcing participation in the cost of new public facilities at the front end of a project, rather than through long-term enhancement of the tax base. In most states, the impact fee must be directly related to the effects of a specific construction or land development project, and must be earmarked to remedy the particular impacts that result from the project.

System development charges, also known as utility expansion charges or extension and improvement charges, are associated with specific facility improvements and are often levied on new developments after the improvements are constructed. Their intent is to enable a community to achieve improvements in advance of growth, while placing an equitable portion of the cost on those properties which later develop and make use of the improvements that were built into the system.

Among the various other approaches which may be considered for rate stabilization or facility purchase provisions are: 1) The sale of existing assets; 2) Mark-up by the community as it "retails" the "wholesale" treatment charge; and 3) The dedication of property taxes which are paid by the treatment plant owner.

CONCLUSION

Making a project financeable means making both the debt and equity conditions competitive with other revenue-based transactions in the market. Privatization must meet accepted conventions of security and return in both the debt and equity markets. The capabilities of the contractors involved to properly build a project and to keep it performing well, technically and financially, are as important as the institutional and contractual aspects of the project.

Additional factors add to the economics of privatization. The profit incentive of the private sector will motivate it to search for additional revenue streams. The production of saleable by-products from the treatment process, and the acceptance of other wastes for treatment at the plant are two ways in which the private sector can generate additional revenues.

Privatization differs from other financing approaches, but if privatization transactions are properly structured, the result may be the most cost-effective alternative in the absence of large grants. The economics of privatization can be significantly improved by using a combination of creative and traditional financing approaches. But to do so, there are a number of areas and issues that must be given appropriate consideration. Because these issues, in areas that include engineering, finance, tax, and law are highly technical, the advice of experienced experts should be sought when a privatization project is undertaken.

Notes

(1)   The areas of expertise that are needed to properly structure a privatization transaction are discussed in the Conclusion.

(2)   The tax benefits available to the private sector when it undertakes privatization opportunities are discussed in Chapter II, The Privatization Concept, and presented in greater detail in Appendix A. These tax benefits include accelerated depreciation, deductibility of interest and investment and energy tax credits.

(3)   "Take-or-pay" is defined in Note (1) of Chapter VII.

(4)   One of the purposes of this book is to provide readers with an understanding of IDBs, but not to cover the specific opportunities and limitations of IDB financing. The reader contemplating the use of IDBs is advised to seek the assistance of qualified professional advisors for a thorough investigation of the requirements for this, as well as other, types of financing.

(5)   Hough, Wesley C., and Peterson, John E., *"Selection and Use of Financial Advisory Services"*, *Governmental Finance*, March, 1984.

VII LEGAL ISSUES

If a privatization transaction is to be properly structured, adequate consideration must be given to both the state and local laws which can influence the approach, and to the various contractual issues related to the design, financing, construction and operation of the facilities.

It is extremely important to involve legal advisors as early as possible. Enabling state legislation is often required to create an environment conducive to the privatization concept. Existing statutes and ordinances will undoubtedly have to be considered, and the rights, responsibilities and remedies of both the public and private sector partners in the transaction need to be thoroughly understood. Once the first privatization project in a state is completed, legal guidelines or references for other projects will be established.

The degree and types of legal issues which will have to be resolved for privatization to be successfully implemented will vary from project to project. This chapter provides an overview of the issues likely to be encountered in the planning and structuring of a privatization approach. Many of the initial issues focus on the statutory authority of privatization in a particular location. These issues are presented in the form of questions that must be answered to determine the viability of privatization, or as legislative changes needed to make the privatization viable.

After these issues are addressed, other representative elements of a privatization transaction needing the attention of legal counsel are presented. These include documentation such as design, engineering and construction contracts, service agreements, operation and maintenance (O&M) contracts, financing agreements, and labor considerations. Each transaction will have special features, some of which may require special documents.

STATUTORY AUTHORITY ISSUES

The issues presented below do not apply to all privatization projects, but are meant to be representative of the legal issues that should receive consideration and evaluation early in a privatization approach. This material has been adapted from work performed for Arthur Young by LeBoeuf, Lamb, Leiby & MacRae as part of a privatization study conducted for the State of Utah and Salt Lake City.

- Does the state, or a political subdivision thereof, have the authority to issue bonds for purposes of financing the acquisition and construction of water and wastewater treatment facilities by a private party?
  - Would the issuance of bonds for such purposes be subject to limitations or procedures relating to public debt imposed by the state's constitution?
- Under state law, do public authorities or other government entities have the authority to enter into long-term contracts for water and wastewater treatment and disposal services?
  - Can the present governing body of a public authority contractually bind future governing bodies for such services?
  - Under a contract between a public authority and a private party, can or must payment for services be limited to a special source, fund or revenue stream?
  - Will such service contracts be characterized as "public debt" under state law, thereby requiring compliance by public authorities with certain constitutionally-imposed limitations or procedures, prior to entering into such contracts?
  - Under such service contracts, will a public authority's contractual obligation to pay be subject to annual appropriation of funds in its budgeting process?
  - May such contracts be entered into on a "take-or-pay" (1) basis?
- To provide revenues for amounts due under contracts with private party owner/operators, are public authorities authorized to assess user charges?
  - Is the amount of such an assessment limited by state law? (i.e., Could it be high enough to cover all debt service on bonds used to finance water and wastewater treatment facilities as well as the operating and maintenance expenses of such facilities?)

- • Is the public authority's contractual promise to assess charges for such purposes beyond the scope of its authority or a lending of its credit?
- • Is an assessment for such purposes a legitimate service charge or a tax?
- • Does a public authority have the power to mandate that its residents hook up to the new collection system?

- ● Do public authorities have the authority to convey existing water and wastewater treatment facilities to private parties? If not, what procedures should be followed?

- ● Do public authorities have the authority to contract for the future purchase of water and wastewater treatment facilities from private party owners? If so, in what form must such contracts be? (e.g., An option to purchase, or a commitment to purchase?)

- ● Do public authorities have an appropriate sewer use ordinance that, among other things, controls the quality of the influent into the system?

- ● Can a municipality use its powers of eminent domain to acquire property and easements for use by the private firm?

- ● Can the municipality use its powers of eminent domain to take the completed facility from a private owner? Can a municipality waive its power to do so?

Some of these issues warrant further discussion. Assume that a particular city has the authority to contract with a private owner/operator for sewage treatment services. It is a common rule of municipal law that a city council may not enter into a contract which extends beyond the term for which its members were elected unless the subject matter of the contract is business or proprietary in nature, rather than legislative or governmental. Court cases in Utah and California support the conclusion that sewage treatment is an exercise of the business or proprietary power of local government. Therefore, unless expressly prohibited under local ordinances or other statutes, "a long-term contract between a city and a private party owner/operator of a sewage treatment facility will not be deemed an unreasonable restraint on future governing bodies of the city if the subject matter of the contract is necessary, the need urgent and the term comparable to the need." (2)

Legislation prohibiting long-term contracts would deter private sector firms from entering into privatization transactions, because they would have no guarantees that the amount of time needed to attain the expected economic benefits would be met. There are, for example, minimum time periods required to claim and retain certain tax credits and deductions. While five years would typically be the minimum service contract period, a contract of fifteen to twenty years would be more desirable to the private sector. Also, holders of the bonds issued to finance a project would require assurances that key aspects, such as revenue flows from service charges, would be "life of the bond." Because laws limiting the length of the contract period are often imposed at the state level, some states have already passed legislation to allow for extended contracting in privatization transactions. Utah is one of several states that have recently passed laws to enable these long-term service agreements. The Utah Privatization Act gives cities and counties the authority to enter into long-term service contracts with the private owner/operators of water and wastewater facilities. The full text of this Act is presented in Appendix B.

REGULATORY ISSUES

- What is the extent of jurisdiction, if any, of the state public utilities commission over the construction and operation of a water or wastewater treatment facility, over the terms of service between a public authority and the private owner of a facility; and over the contract rate charged by the private owner under the service contract? Being classified as a public utility may affect the tax benefits available to a private sector firm. (3)
  - Does state utility law require obtaining any document, permit, certificate or authorization prior to construction or operation of such facilities?

STATE AND LOCAL TAX ISSUES

Each state and community has its own laws regarding tax issues. Because these issues so directly affect the economics of a privatization transaction, they should be investigated carefully. Representative legal issues pertaining to state and local taxes include the following:

- Will state income taxes be applicable to income earned by the private owner?

- Will state sales taxes be applicable to purchases of materials and labor for the construction of the facility? To the service charges payable by the municipality?

- If desirable, will a property tax exemption be available for the facility?

ANTITRUST LIABILITIES

An issue that is often raised about privatization is whether the contractual relationship between a public authority and the private party owner of a water or wastewater treatment facility gives rise to liability on the part of either the public authority, the private party or both under federal and state antitrust laws. Based on legal analyses performed by counsel in privatization work to date, it appears that it is possible for municipalities wishing to undertake privatization to be exempted from the application of antitrust laws under the state action doctrine. (4)

PUBLIC CONTRACTING PROCESS

- To what extent do state and local procurement laws apply to the construction or operation of water and wastewater treatment facilities?
  - Do laws require a certain selection process for the owner/operator of such facilities?
  - Do such laws restrict the terms of the service contract between a public authority and the owner/operator of such facilities?
  - Do such laws apply to the future acquisition of the contemplated facilities by a public authority?

- What is the impact of state and local laws on labor contracts and public health and safety during the construction and operation of water and wastewater treatment facilities?

- What state and local land use and construction statutes, regulations and ordinances apply to the construction or operation of water and wastewater treatment facilities (e.g., siting, zoning, public rights-of-way, franchise requirements)?

- What federal and state environmental laws apply to the construction and operation of water and wastewater treatment facilities?

Consideration should also be given to any existing contracts to which the municipality may be committed. Whether the commitments are labor contracts or contracts for materials and supplies, it should be determined if transfer to a private sector firm or handling in some other manner is a fair and equitable alternative for all parties concerned.

LABOR CONSIDERATIONS

As the community begins to develop its plan to implement a privatization approach, the existence of union contracts or civil service issues that would prohibit, restrict or influence the conditions of private operation of the facility must be considered. Depending on the restrictions and conditions which exist, a labor contract, if needed, should be appropriately structured. It may, for example, be especially beneficial if the private sector firm incorporates some of the more experienced and qualified members of the public work force into its own ranks. However, there may be legal constraints that prohibit municipal employees from taking on this role. If no constraints exist, and a private sector labor contract which incorporates public work force employees is structured, then certain employment conditions and contract provisions must be included to protect employee interests and benefits.

OPERATOR CERTIFICATION

Investigations should be made of the state and local requirements for private operators of wastewater treatment facilities, both on the individual and company level. It may be necessary for certain criteria to be met before private sector plant operation can begin. There may even be qualifications regarding the amount of operating experience that the private sector firm would need to have to even propose on a project. Knowing such stipulations in advance could save both the private and public sectors time and effort later in the privatization implementation process.

Once these and other legal issues have been considered and addressed, any steps that are necessary to ease the implementation of privatization should be taken. These steps may range from the review of existing contracts to the passage of state legislation or of local laws and ordinances to enable the implementation of the privatization approach. The knowledge and insights obtained through the investigation of these legal issues will be needed to structure the documents that will shape and drive the privatization transaction.

DOCUMENTATION

Preparing appropriate documentation is an essential part of structuring the privatization transaction. Each transaction requires a service agreement, a contract to provide for operation and maintenance (O&M) and a financing agreement. Site-specific circumstances may warrant additional documents. Figure VII-1 illustrates the contracts, agreements and relationships in a typical privatization arrangement, assuming the issuance of tax-exempt debt. The functions of each contract and parties to the contracts are summarized in Figure VII-2. In addition to the agreements discussed below, a privatization transaction may include a ground lease and equity and construction agreements.

THE SERVICE CONTRACT

The service contract is an agreement between a municipality and the privatizer to provide treatment services. It is the principal document in any privatization transaction. This contract outlines the terms of a privatization partnership, and should include any provisions which protect the interests of both partners in the transaction. The terms of a service contract, most likely to be a version of the take-or-pay agreement, will provide the principal credit support for the project. The municipality will establish and collect rates to produce revenues for payments to the private firm, which are stipulated in the service contract. Variations may exist, such as where the "privatizer" will directly bill to and collect from the system users.

Also included in a service contract is the service charge schedule that the private sector party will charge the municipality. This schedule is likely to include rate escalation clauses, which often will be tied to labor, power and material indices and force majeure events. A purchase option to allow the municipality, under clearly laid-out circumstances, to purchase the facility from the private sector party, is also likely to be part of the service contract.

The length of contract period is one of the major provisions of the service contract. In most cases, the private sector will want to be assured

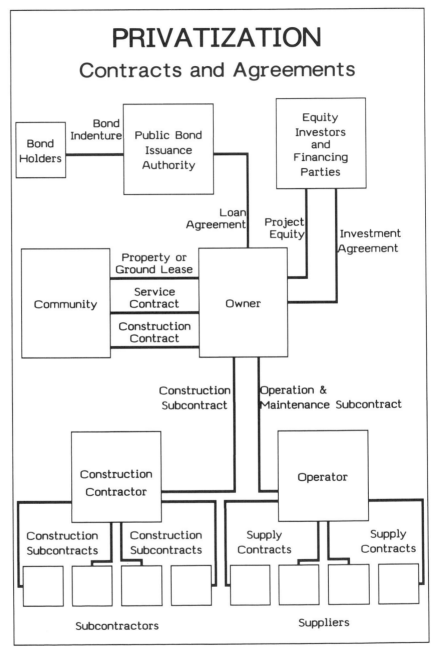

Figure VII-1

CONTRACT	PARTIES	REPRESENTATIVE FUNCTIONS
Investment & Loan Agreement	— Owner/Financiers — Owner/Public Authority	Establishes terms of loan, investments and mortgage lien.
Bond Indenture	— Bond Issuer/Bond Holders	Establishes terms of bond issue.
Ground Lease	— Owner/Community	Establishes land lease, access, and construction constraints, if any.
Service Contract	— Owner/Community	Establishes an agreement to provide treatment services, treatment standards, influent and effluent requirements, etc.; a service contract may include an engineering agreement.
Construction Contract	— Owner/Community	Identifies requirements re: access to public properties, rights of way, other legal issues, time schedules and manner of construction, etc.
Construction Subcontract	— Owner/Contractor	Identifies construction terms and schedules; relationships with subcontractors.
Operation & Maintenance Subcontract	— Owner/Operator	Establishes terms of operations, performance standards, maintenance requirements, penalties, etc.
Construction Subcontracts	— Contractor/Subcontractors	Establishes construction requirements, schedules, etc.
Supply Contracts	— Operator/Supplier	Provides for supply deliveries and payments.

Figure VII-2

of maximizing its tax benefits, and will ask for the stipulation of a contract period of at least fifteen to twenty years. The municipality, however, may want to protect its interests by specifying the conditions for termination of the contract. One such condition may be if the private sector is unable to provide the necessary treatment to meet the requirements set forth in the National Pollution Discharge Elimination System Permit. The requirements of the debt side of the transaction will also influence the length of contract term. Other aspects of the service contract which relate to the tax benefits of privatization transactions are discussed in Appendix A. Included in that Appendix is a discussion of the six criteria established in the Deficit Reduction Act of 1984 for the Internal Revenue Service's determination of whether a valid service contract and the resulting tax benefits exist.

Another issue to be addressed in the service agreement is the allocation of liabilities and fines. In most cases, the privatizer will be responsible for operational difficulties and the quality of the effluent. However, the private sector's liability will be dependent on the municipality meeting its responsibilities in prohibiting excessive or unacceptable influent loadings. Allowable influent loadings should be negotiated between the municipality and the private sector firm, and stipulated in the service agreement.

The service contract may also include an engineering agreement, to allow the owner to provide or subcontract design and engineering services for the project.

THE O&M CONTRACT

If the private sector owner of the facility is not the operator, the operation and maintenance agreement (O&M), or the operating lease between owner and operator, should be carefully scrutinized by the municipality.

Many communities across the country are contracting with private sector firms for the O&M of their wastewater treatment facilities. The same issues that make up an O&M agreement in those situations will apply to contracts between owners and operators in privatization transactions. Figure VII-3 contains a representative table of contents from an O&M contract for a wastewater treatment facility.

Relative to privatization, the principal issues of this contract involve the extent of operator liability to the owner, which extends indirectly to

REPRESENTATIVE AGREEMENT FOR
CONTRACT OPERATION AND MAINTENANCE SERVICES
FOR A WASTEWATER TREATMENT FACILITY

1. Declaration of Participants' Intent

2. Identification of Facility

3. Length of Contract Period

4. Scope of Services

   a. Employment of Existing Personnel
   b. Record Keeping
   c. Security
   d. Preventive Maintenance
   e. Enforcement of Existing Warranties and Guarantees
   f. NPDES Testing and Laboratory Requirements
   g. Operational Meetings
   h. Compliance with State and Federal Regulations
   i. Compliance with NPDES Discharge Requirements
   j. O&M Expenditures
   k. Liability for Fines and Civil Penalties
   l. Staffing
   m. Modifications to Existing Structures
   n. Odor Control
   o. Sludge Management
   p. Buy "local"
   q. Training Programs
      — Contractor's Employees
      — Municipal Employees
   r. Budgeting Requirements

5. Municipal Responsiblities
   a. Quality and Quantity of Influent
   b. New Hook-ups; Charges
   c. Pretreatment

6. Compensation

7. Liability Provisions

8. Insurance

9. Scope Changes

10. Municipal Access to Facility

11. Additional Construction

12. Ownership of New Capital Facilities

13. Contract Renewal Option

14. Termination of Contract

15. Municipal Insurance

16. Responsibilities Under Force Majeure Conditions

Figure VII-3

the municipality. A municipality may want to review this contract, paying special attention to the adequacy of insurance coverage and guarantees for meeting treatment requirements. If the operator designs and constructs the facility for an owner, the municipality should also review the construction contract with regard to design standards, completion guarantees and other matters.

THE TAX-EXEMPT FINANCING AGREEMENT

In many privatization transactions, tax-exempt financing will be used to finance most of the costs of construction. Federal tax laws strictly regulate tax-exempt borrowing. Therefore, an unconditional opinion by bond counsel as to the tax exemption status of interest on the debt is generally required.

The financing agreement and trust indenture will include the financial covenants and requirements imposed on the owner. These will also be reflected in the service agreement, particularly as related to service charge provisions, and to capital or O&M conditions that affect project economies.

Notes

(1)   In a "take-or-pay" contract a minimum payment is stipulated. For example in a wastewater treatment privatization take-or-pay contract the minimum payment would be stipulated for treatment of 5 mgd of wastewater. If the community, on a given day, provided only 3 million gallons per day to the treatment facility, it would still be required to pay the minimum payment. Even if no wastewater were delivered to the facility, the community would still have to pay the minimum fee.

(2)   Memorandum from LeBoeuf, Lamb, Leiby & MacRae to Arthur Young contained in *PRIVATIZATION: A Legal Analysis,* Prepared for the State of Utah and Salt Lake City by Arthur Young, November, 1983. The memorandum states that "The state action doctrine...generally exempts from the coverage of the federal antitrust laws 'anticompetitive conduct engaged in as an act of government by the State as sovereign, or, by its subdivisions, pursuant to state policy to displace competition with regulation or monopoly public service.'"

(3)   Appendix A contains a discussion of the effects of Public Utility Property classification on the tax benefits of privatization transactions.

(4)   LeBoeuf, Lamb, Leiby & MacRae memorandum cited above.

VIII REGULATORY CONCERNS: FEDERAL AND STATE POLICY ISSUES AND ROLES

"The Federal government developed [the 1972 Clean Water Act] programs and regulations because they believed the states could not effectively do so. Now that the proliferation of federal regulation has made them complicated and cumbersome, the programs are being handed back to the states."

Jackie Swigart
Secretary
Department of Natural Resources
& Environmental Protection
Kentucky

Privatization necessarily involves policy decisions at all levels of government: federal, state and local. Once these are made, each level can determine the extent to which it will support, take an active role in, or otherwise become involved with the privatization process. So far, each time we have made reference to the public side of the privatization partnership, we have discussed the local community and its policy decision regarding whether or not to take on a privatization project. In this chapter the roles of federal and state government in privatization will be considered.

Reduction in the federal funding of treatment facilities raised the issues of who would pay for facilities, how they would be financed and what role the federal government would subsequently play. However, other federal actions affected the development of the privatization concept.

The indirect role of the federal government in the development of the privatization concept is apparent in the passage of tax laws which enhance the private sector's basic business opportunity in the provision of treatment services. However, through the multitude of agencies which carry out the directives of its different branches, the federal government affects privatization in a number of other ways. Indirectly, it has encouraged the development of privatization through changes to the U.S. Environmental Protection Agency's Construction Grants Program, and it has exerted additional influence over its application and structuring of privatization transactions through directives of the Office of Management and Budget.

OMB INVOLVEMENT—SAFEGUARDING PREVIOUS FEDERAL INVESTMENTS

Since 1970, Congress has appropriated more than $35 billion for the establishment of wastewater treatment systems across the United States, primarily through the Construction Grants Program, administered by the U.S. Environmental Protection Agency. Many of these treatment systems, either currently or in the future, will need further investments for expansion, modification, upgrading or rehabilitation. A discussion of the federal policies involved in privatization transactions as they affect those federally funded projects would not be complete without consideration of the Office of Management and Budget (OMB). Suppose that as part of a privatization transaction, a municipality wishes to attract private investment either to purchase or make further capital investments in a facility which was constructed with a grant from the U.S. Environmental Protection Agency. Can this be done, and if so, what is the municipality's (grantee's) obligation to repay the federal government?

Insight to the answer is provided by OMB in Circular A-102 (1). Attachment M to A-102 contains the standard forms for applying for federal assistance. A grant applicant must give assurance and certify, with respect to the grant, that he "will not dispose of or encumber its title or other interests in the site and facilities during the period of Federal interest or while the Government holds bonds, whichever is the longer."

While the term "period of Federal interest" is not defined, one interpretation may be that it refers to a facility's useful life. If the facility is determined to be at the end of its useful life, then rules in Attachment N, which governs the utilization and disposition of property furnished by the federal government or acquired in whole or in part with federal funds, come into play. In such a case, if the facility has reached the end of its useful life, and the municipality wishes to sell the facility, the municipality must turn over a pro rata share of the proceeds of sale to the federal government. In one recent situation, the government estimated the fair market value of a facility and demanded a pro rata share of that amount as its settlement figure. The effect of this directive on the economic attractiveness of privatization transactions should be evaluated on a case-by-case basis. For example, fair market value of an existing facility in need of upgrading, rehabilitation or expansion may be significant. In such cases, rather than have the privatizer attempt to purchase that facility, it would be prudent to explore the concept of leasing the existing facility, with its ownership staying in the hands of the grantee (the municipality). The privatizer would own and operate the necessary system improvements while leasing the existing facility, thus establishing operating control of the entire system.

Under special circumstances, OMB may waive these repayment requirements. (2) If such a waiver is desired, the grantee would first approach the grantor agency. Then, if the agency felt a waiver should be granted, the agency would bring the matter to OMB. According to sources at OMB, the burden of proof to obtain the waiver is on the applicant, who must show, among other specific requirements, that every possible means to finance, refinance or keep the system running has been exhausted. A municipality considering such a transaction should also consider any state government reimbursement requirements if state funding was involved in the project.

PRIVATIZATION: A DRAIN OR AN INFLOW TO THE FEDERAL TREASURY

There has been some heated opposition to the use of the tax benefits in certain types of financing transactions, especially those referred to as "sale-leasebacks." In recent years, existing facilities, such as convention centers, city halls and college dormitories have been sold to taxpaying entities who could claim the tax benefits of ownership, then lease the facilities back to the original tax-exempt owner at a favorable rate which reflected a share of the tax benefits. Many argue that no new construction, jobs or investments result from this type of transaction; only tax benefits that are created at the expense of the Federal Treasury. The 1984 tax act, among other purposes, was designed to curtail "sale/leaseback" abuses.

Privatization is different; it does not utilize "sale/leasebacks" between business and government. It is a business venture, complete with financing, construction and operating risks. Privatization of water and wastewater treatment and resource recovery facilities, among other types of needed capital-intensive ventures, is targeted at creating jobs, building facilities, fostering economic growth and solving environmental problems. Studies have shown that the net result of using tax benefits to foster privatization transactions may be a positive inflow to the Federal Treasury over the life of the project.

Arthur Young performed a financial analysis of a medium-sized wastewater treatment project to determine the economic impact on the Federal Treasury of tax benefits associated with privatization versus the effect to the Treasury if the facility received a 55% federal grant.

This analysis was comprised of two elements: 1) inflows due to taxes paid by the private sector firm on taxable income, which includes service charge, profit on operation and maintenance of the facility and the ultimate sale price of the facility; and 2) outflows due to tax benefits claimed, including tax deductions and investment tax credit. These key assumptions were reviewed with regulatory agencies, industry trade groups and investment banking professionals.

Results showed that, on a net present value basis, there would be a significant cost savings to the Treasury if a project was implemented through privatization rather than through grant funding. It was concluded that "certain projects may actually produce a positive effect on the Treasury in terms of benefits claimed versus taxes paid [by the private sector firms involved] over the life of the [project and service] agreement."(3) Furthermore, short-term effects of privatization include the stimulation of the equipment manufacturing and construction industries and the economic development which typically results from increased treatment capacity. The intent of this analysis was not to suggest that privatization should be used in lieu of grant funding; rather it was to legitimatize privatization as a concept to supplement grant funding as a means of reducing the economic burden on treatment system users. The analysis was prepared and presented at a time when the U.S. House of Representatives and the U.S. Senate were addressing proposed legislation on the use of tax benefits and industrial development bonds for facilities such as privately owned water, wastewater and resource recovery facilities.

Privatization transactions are neither tax gimmicks nor simply a means of providing cheap financing to the public sector. Rather, properly conceived and structured, they are legitimate economic transactions, designed to put the private sector into real business opportunities and to provide communities with badly-needed treatment facilities through the most cost effective form of service delivery.

Some communities will be fortunate enough to receive federal grants for eligible project costs. But, for the thousands of communities that cannot receive this direct federal aid, it seems appropriate as a matter of national policy to make available the indirect aid of the federal tax laws; especially since such aid will not necessarily result in a drain on the treasury, and may in fact have an overall positive effect on the federal, state and local economies.

The U.S. Environmental Protection Agency is currently studying financing alternatives to the Construction Grants Program. These alternatives include privatization. Agency officials recognize that there is not enough money to meet treatment needs through existing grant programs. While privatization is still under study, it appears that the Agency will support any reasonable alternative for the provision of cost effective treatment systems. (4)

A ROLE FOR THE STATE

Perhaps first to feel the effects of the federal funding cutbacks were the state governments. Some states have already established infrastructure financing task force programs and have included new financing alternatives, such as privatization, in their recent capital budget plans. The governors of a number of states have established task forces which specifically address wastewater treatment needs.

Some states, such as California, have already finalized the task force reports. Other states are still progressing through the studies. Among the recommendations contained in the California report is the following:

> Encourage establishing State and local programs and procedures to evaluate privatization's potential in constructing, maintaining and operating infrastructure facilities.

Other states have not been as enthusiastic about the privatization concept. One state received a recommendation from its consultant to delay considering privatization, as it was considered to be too early in the evolution of the concept to make a commitment to the approach.

The State of New York made clear its policy decision regarding privatization in its Five-Year Capital Plan for fiscal years 1984-85 through 1988-89. The discussion of innovative financing mechanisms reads:

> Complete 'privatization' of some facilities may be feasible and even desirable. Under privatization, facilities are owned and operated, and financing arranged, by the private sector. . . .
>
> State agencies considering privatization must examine its cost-effectiveness and cost-benefit against other alternatives.
>
> Also, agencies must establish incentives and oversight mechanisms for private operators to ensure fiscal stability and adequate delivery of services.
>
> Innovative financing by local governments may ultimately reduce burdens on the State by reducing overall needs for financing. Resource recovery and sewage treatment plants can be financed by privatization or leveraged leasing mechanisms.

Policy decisions must be made at the state level as to the degree to which the state will assist communities in meeting local treatment needs. Because privatization is rapidly being accepted by many local communities as a viable financing alternative, states will have to make clear their positions on a number of privatization issues, including contract terms, rate regulation, the procurement of privatization services and the potential reservation of allotments for industrial development bond financings.

The degree of involvement on the part of an individual state government will vary. At a minimum, states must have an understanding of the concept, because it can be anticipated that communities in need of facilities and the private sector will look to the state not only on legal matters, but also on regulatory issues such as the state's enforcement attitude and procedures related to the various permits to be secured.

Permits which will need to be obtained at the Federal and/or state level by groups building and operating a treatment plant may include the following:

- National Pollution Discharge Elimination System.
- Prevention of Significant Deterioration Permit (if discharges are made into the air).
- Generator Identification Number (under the Resource Conservation and Recovery Act).
- A Contractor's license.

Many state governments and associations are making significant efforts to understand privatization. The Association of State and Interstate Water Pollution Control Administrators and the Council of State Governments are two of the groups that are educating their members on the privatization concept. In addition to understanding this concept, states must decide the extent to which they will control or influence privatization. If legislation is needed to enable the concept to go forward, that legislation could be the vehicle through which states control procurement procedures, influence the allocation of risks between the different partners in the transaction and establish community oversight programs.

Figure VIII-1 depicts different levels of state participation in privatization. Understanding the privatization concept is the minimum level of action that should be required of every state. Beyond that, the degree of state involvement in a privatization program will vary. A state-supported implementation program, which is shown in Figure VIII-2 and discussed below, presents many options for states wishing to actively support privatization as an alternative for communities to consider.

States in which local communities undertake privatization projects may have to take on some responsibility related to protecting the interests of the public sector, without jeopardizing the private firm's interest level. The level of responsibility to be taken on by the state may depend on the existing degree of state involvement in local affairs. In its privatization legislation, the State of New Jersey (See Appendix C) included provisions regarding recommended procedures for soliciting proposals, selecting qualified groups and negotiating and awarding contracts. These provisions include state review of privatization contracts by the Department of Environmental Protection, the Department of Community Affairs and the Public Advocate.

REPRESENTATIVE PRIVATIZATION STATE ACTIONS

CLASSIFICATION	CLASSIFICATION DESCRIPTION	REPRESENTATIVE STATES ACTIONS
Active Promotion	State has taken definitive actions to show support and promote privatization.	**New Jersey** — Sponsored conceptual level feasibility study. — Distributed report to all communities on U.S. EPA Needs list. — Incorporated Concept into proposed Infrastructure Bank program. — Held meetings with interested privatizers. — Developed legislation. **Utah** — Funded part of statewide feasibility study. — Held seminar for state and local officials. — Has advertised a "Request for Qualifications" for privatization from interested private sector firms. — Passed the Utah Privatization Act.
Emphasizing Privatization Education and Enabling Legislation	States have made information on privatization readily available, want local officials to be aware of and understand the concept.	**Tennessee** — Passed legislation to allow long-term service agreement. — Has budgeted funds for a contract with a local university which may be used for preparation of generic, statewide privatization material and statewide seminars. — Privatization was main topic at State Municipal League Seminar.
Privatization Awareness	Cabinet-level officials and/or personnel from involved state departments have been provided with education on the privatization concept; further actions may be pending.	— More than 20 states - all sections of the country.

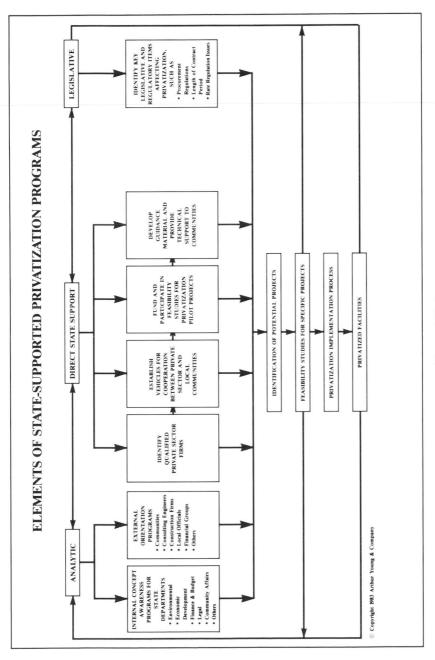

ELEMENTS OF STATE-SUPPORTED PRIVATIZATION PROGRAMS

ANALYTIC

INTERNAL CONCEPT AWARENESS PROGRAMS FOR STATE DEPARTMENTS
• Environmental
• Economic Development
• Finance & Budget
• Legal
• Community Affairs
• Others

EXTERNAL ORIENTATION PROGRAMS
• Communities
• Consulting Engineers
• Construction Firms
• Local Officials
• Financial Groups
• Others

DIRECT STATE SUPPORT

IDENTIFY QUALIFIED PRIVATE SECTOR FIRMS

ESTABLISH VEHICLES FOR COOPERATION BETWEEN PRIVATE SECTOR AND LOCAL COMMUNITIES

FUND AND PARTICIPATE IN FEASIBILITY STUDIES FOR PRIVATIZATION PILOT PROJECTS

DEVELOP GUIDANCE MATERIAL AND PROVIDE TECHNICAL SUPPORT TO COMMUNITIES

LEGISLATIVE

IDENTIFY KEY LEGISLATIVE AND REGULATORY ITEMS AFFECTING PRIVATIZATION, SUCH AS
• Procurement Regulations
• Length of Contract Period
• Rate Regulation Issues

IDENTIFICATION OF POTENTIAL PROJECTS

FEASIBILITY STUDIES FOR SPECIFIC PROJECTS

PRIVATIZATION IMPLEMENTATION PROCESS

PRIVATIZED FACILITIES

© Copyright 1983 Arthur Young & Company

Figure VIII-2

A very important determination to be made at the state level is whether or not a state's public utilities commission (PUC), or its equivalent, will have jurisdiction over the project and the rate structure associated with it. PUC intervention could affect the tax benefits claimed by a private firm and will influence vendor interest. In New Jersey, given the oversight program described above, the policy decision was made to insulate privatization transactions from PUC rate regulation. Appendix A presents a detailed explanation of the potential impact of rate regulation on tax benefits.

ELEMENTS OF A STATE SUPPORTED PROGRAM

Many actions can be taken at the state level to provide a positive privatization environment, as shown in the chart in Figure VIII-2. These possible actions can be divided into three categories: Analytic; Direct Support; and Legislative. These categories, as well as many of the actions listed within each, are interrelated. While some actions must necessarily come before others, there is no standard order in which these actions should be taken.

Analytic Activities

Analytic activities at the state level involve privatization education programs for both state and external personnel. Internal education programs for all agencies and departments that would normally be involved in capital intensive public projects should be developed. In some cases, initial reactions to privatization are influenced by a lack of understanding of the concept. By explaining the privatization concept to departments such as economic development and finance & budget, the staffs will consider privatization as an alternative approach for helping to meet local community needs. Examples of how some state departments can benefit from involvement and participation in the formulation of privatization strategies are given below:

Environmental Protection: Environmental protection departments know first-hand that available funds do not come close to meeting the needs for facilities. Agencies that understand the benefits of privatization can make their communities and their engineering advisors aware of this financing alternative.

Economic Development: Charged with directing the economic growth of a state, this agency has insights into the needs of particular areas and industries, and can incorporate the privatization alternative when evaluating resources and needs. By providing needed treatment facilities, privatization may enable development in an area that would otherwise remain depressed. In some cases, the state economic development authorities may be the issuing agencies for the industrial development bonds to finance projects.

Finance & Budget: More than any other state agency, the finance & budget departments understand the financial difficulties faced by local governments. Consideration of the privatization alternative may enable them to provide financially-troubled communities with a full range of funding alternatives, and through the support of privatization, foster growth of a community's tax base.

Legal: In certain instances, laws must be changed or put into place to implement privatization. The determination as to whether laws in a particular state need amendment must be made with both a complete knowledge of existing state law and an understanding of privatization. State attorney general offices can provide necessary legal information, but only with an understanding of the privatization concept will they be in a position to best judge which issues are significantly related to the implementation of privatization.

Community Affairs: Public support of a privatization project is an important element in the project's success. If the community affairs department understands privatization and the benefits it offers, it can take a lead role in public education and public relations activities.

Organizing educational programs for audiences external to state government can also be beneficial. These programs can be aimed at those who would play a role in the privatization process. As shown in Figure VIII-2, the audiences would include officials from local communities, consulting engineers, construction firms and financial groups. One of the main issues to be addressed in these programs is that privatization will change, but not eliminate, the traditional roles played by these groups.

Privatization seminars can be vehicles for cooperation between the private sector and local communities. These can be sponsored through the departments discussed above. Staffs of the separate departments can work together to pair communities in need of facilities with private sector firms interested in privatization. State-sponsored seminars can also be held, allowing private sector firms to present privatization information to representatives and officials from local communities. These seminars would open a line of communication between those in need of facilities and those with the capabilities to provide them. For example, at the Tennessee Municipal League's annual conference in 1983, the entire theme was privatization. Presentations included "The Municipal Role in State Growth," "The Privatization of Public Facilities" and "Privatizing of Public Facilities and Services in Tennessee."

Direct State Support

State governments can support privatization in a number of ways. The aim of any support activity undertaken by state government would be to simplify the privatization process for local communities. In a case where the state participates in a state-wide privatization feasibility study, the aim would be to identify and remedy, on a state level, the issues which could hinder or otherwise obstruct the privatization process. In addition to feasibility studies, there are other activities that the state government can undertake to provide local communities with direct support. One way is for the state to develop a list of pre-qualified firms that have the credentials and experience to participate in privatization projects.

An excellent example of direct state support is the state-wide feasibility study. Communities in a state wishing to determine the feasibility of privatization can draw on the knowledge and insights provided by this study. Actions on certain legal issues identified in the state-wide study can be taken early in the local privatization process making the path clearer for communities wishing to pursue privatization opportunities.

In January, 1983, the State of Utah and Salt Lake City co-sponsored a study to determine the feasibility of using private sector monies to finance public sewage treatment plants. This project was unique because it was the first privatization effort in the state, and it was also the first jointly funded privatization effort between a state government and a local community in the country. Other states are now pursuing similar paths.

Findings of the study related to both the feasibility of projects specific to Salt Lake City and state-wide privatization issues. A state-wide seminar for communities in need of facilities was part of this consulting project. For the specific projects analyzed, privatization was found to save a significant percentage in financing costs as compared to both traditional means and the somewhat unique financing approach of "pay-as-you-go." State-wide conclusions included the following:

- There is extensive interest on the part of the private sector to participate in a privatization transaction. Twenty-five proposals were received from firms responding to a national notice regarding privatization opportunities in the State of Utah.

- The State Division of Environmental Health, the state's environmental protection department, is supportive of the concept.

- Certain state laws had to be changed to allow privatization to take place. The legal issues that needed to be and, subsequently, were, addressed in the State of Utah included the following:
  - Cities must receive authorization to enter into full service contracts with private firms for sewage treatment.
  - The private sector firm in a privatization transaction must be exempted from the definition of "a utility" to avoid a loss of tax benefits and to enable the use of Industrial Development Bonds for project financing.
  - Cities must be protected from potential antitrust liabilities that may be considered to arise from privatization.(5)

Another example of direct state support and involvement is a state developing generic privatization material such as Requests for Qualifications and/or Proposals (RFQ and/or RFP) and contract outlines, which communities can tailor to their specific needs. Such an approach will reduce the time and cost necessary for a community to pursue privatization. A generic RFQ will set out the minimum acceptable experience for bidders on a privatization project. For wastewater treatment facilities, there may be a requirement regarding prior state certification for operators, or previous experience operating a treatment plant in that particular state. The generic RFP will include information regarding procurement and contracting. (A more detailed description of the typical RFQ and RFP is presented in Chapter III, An Orderly Approach for Success). State governments could also develop lists of pre-qualified firms that have the credentials and experience to participate in privatization projects.

LEGISLATIVE ACTIONS

Legislative actions can be taken at the state level to support privatization. Generally, issues that need to be resolved at the state level include the ability of municipalities to enter into long term contracts, appropriate procurement methods and rate regulation provisions. These issues, as well as the Utah Privatization Act, are discussed in detail in Chapter VII. Some examples of states that are taking legislative action with regard to privatization are presented here.

In Georgia, legislation was recently enacted to expand the powers of an existing authority, allowing it to assist in financing water and wastewater projects. The legislation empowers the authority to investigate the feasibility of private ownership and operation of facilities for possible lease-back arrangements with the local governments and/or state. (6)

In Tennessee, a 1983 act authorizes municipalities to enter into contracts, leases and lease-purchase agreements for terms of up to 40 years with respect to capital improvement property. (7) This legislation allows municipalities to enter into long-term contracts with private sector firms for various types of privatization transactions, including wastewater treatment.

Legislation making possible the privatization of wastewater treatment plants was recently introduced in Alabama, and a coordinated effort was made to get the legislation passed. As previously described, the City of Auburn has undertaken a program for the privatization of a 5.4 mgd wastewater treatment plant. The City Attorney concluded that, to allow this solution to Auburn's wastewater treatment needs, it would be necessary to develop appropriate legislation. A program was begun that included briefing local legislators on the concept of privatization. Letters were sent to legislators and mayors on the state environmental department priority list for wastewater treatment facility contruction, briefly explaining the concept and Auburn's particular needs. The letters urged favorable treatment of legislation allowing the privatization of wastewater treatment facilities.

The State of New Jersey recently introduced legislation concerning long-term contracts for wastewater treatment privatization. Among other things, this proposed legislation establishes a procedure for the negotiating, awarding and review of privatization service contracts. A copy of the act is contained in Appendix C.

Passing legislation often requires a substantial amount of time. If a state determines that privatization can help it meet its needs, state officials should begin any legislative processes as quickly as possible, so that privatization projects are not unnecessarily delayed, and so that attention can be focused on the most appropriate methods to protect the public interests.

Notes

(1)   *Office of Management and Budget, Circular A-102 (Revised), "Uniform Requirements for Assistance to State and Local Governments,"* January, 1981. The reader should note that Circular A-102 is being revised.

(2)   The circular states that ''...in the interest of keeping conformity to the maximum extent, deviations from the requirements of this circular will be permitted only in exceptional cases.''

(3)   *"Privatization of Wastewater Treatment Facilities,"* Testimony presented by Harvey Goldman, Partner, Arthur Young & Company, before the U.S. House of Representatives Committee on Public Works and Transportation, Subcommittee on Water Resources, November, 1983.

(4)   *"Feds 'bless' privatization,"* Engineering News-Record, December 15, 1983.

(5)   Arthur Young, *PRIVATIZATION: A Comprehensive Analysis,* Prepared for Salt Lake City and the State of Utah, November, 1983,

(6)   Evjen, Lowell, *"A Bond Bank for Water and Sewer Facilities,"* Stretching Dollars to Strengthen Infrastructure, Proceedings from a conference presented on April 29-30, 1983, sponsored by the Eastern Regional Conference of The Council of State Governments, in cooperation with the Southern Legislative Conference of The Council of State Governments.

(7)   Information provided to Arthur Young by the Tennessee Municipal League. Capital improvement property is defined in the bill as ''any real or tangible personal property needed for a governmental purpose and having a useful life of one year or more, and any real or tangible personal property with respect to which capital outlay notes can be legally authorized and issued by a municipality.''

IX CONCLUSION: SPIRIT OF PARTNERSHIP

Several factors contribute to the success of privatization. These have to do with the project, the community which will receive the service and the way in which the public/private partners approach the privatization transaction. The key factors include the following:

- The Need for the Project
- The Project's Economic Viability
- Public Acceptance
- An Appropriate Legal Environment
- A Comprehensive Feasibility Study
- An Orderly and Controlled Implementation
- A Spirit of Partnership

Project Need: Privatization is a means of service delivery. Without a true need for the service, there is no need for privatization. The degree to which the need exists will directly influence the success of privatization.

When searching for communities for privatization projects, need is one of the key factors. In the case of a wastewater treatment facility, a community that is far down on the U.S. EPA Needs List and has very little, if any, chance for a federal grant may be a good candidate for privatization. Communities strongly desiring a project, but not having the financial wherewithal to finance it, may be receptive to alternative financing approaches. Privatization may also be attractive to financially sophisticated communities confident of their ability to control the implementation of a public/private partnership.

Economic Viability: An economically viable privatization project will meet the goals of both public and private sector partners. The public sector wants reliable and timely service delivery at a cost which is lower than it could otherwise obtain. The private sector wants a fair return on its investment. Meeting both these needs on an equitable basis is at the heart of privatization.

Privatization requires that a public sector partner contribute the time and effort needed to ensure that its interests are well protected. In structuring the privatization approach, the private sector should also take into consideration that the savings in user fees should be substantial enough to make the public sector's effort worthwhile.

Public Acceptance: Public officials have the responsibility of acting in behalf of their constituencies, who often make their likes and dislikes well known. Public officials will support privatization concepts if they believe that these concepts are supported by the people they represent. For some communities, privatization concepts may be completely new, and a lack of understanding may prevent the community from clearly seeing the benefits available. A program to educate the public about privatization and inform it of the specific benefits of the privatization project being considered is essential for public sector acceptance and the success of the project.

The public acceptance of privatization is more likely to take place in cities and towns that have previously turned to the private sector for the delivery of services that were traditionally the responsibility of the public sector. Municipalities that are satisfied with the services provided by private sector contractors will be more willing to entertain thoughts of full-scale privatization projects, including the ownership of treatment facilities.

An Appropriate Legal Environment: Privatization can only be successful if contractual relationships and long-term commitments are established. Municipalities in states with legal environments conducive to the concept are likely to see the first round of privatization projects. A ready environment is one in which no legislative changes are needed to implement privatization. Putting legislation into place is often a time-consuming process. Even when the identification of the legal issues affecting privatization is a part of the initial feasibility study, the passage of enabling legislation for privatization may take a relatively long time. This is one reason why efforts to educate state personnel about the concept should be made early in the privatization process. Once state government personnel can recognize the value and benefits of privatization, they are more likely to actively encourage, support and foster its development.

A Comprehensive Feasibility Study: The first step in carrying out a privatization approach is to determine if the concept is feasible for a particular project. As discussed in Chapter III, An Orderly Approach for Success, there are a number of areas which should be carefully addressed to determine the feasibility of a particular privatization project. These are: Needs, Technologies, Vendor Interest, Risks & Benefits, Financing, Legal Issues and Regulatory Agency Issues.

Conducting a proper privatization analysis, structuring the transaction and planning implementation requires technical competence in a number of areas. These areas are highlighted on the following page in Figure IX-1.

An Orderly and Controlled Implementation: Privatization will be successful only if the implementation is appropriately planned and properly carried out. Privatization must be thoroughly analyzed as to its feasibility for a particular project, and once feasibility is established, its implementation must be well thought out and executed. There are a number of areas which need to be addressed during the privatization process. If a key issue is omitted or otherwise short-changed, the project's success will suffer. Any lack of thoroughness or care in analysis and planning may result in haphazard and unsuccessful implementation.

A Spirit of Partnership: In structuring a privatization approach, a responsibility of the public officials to their constituents is to ensure that the community will receive the service in a timely and cost-effective manner, and that public health will be protected. Public officials also have a responsibility to the private sector firm to allow it a fair return on its investment and a reasonable profit from the business venture. The

PRIVATIZATION SKILL AREAS

SKILL AREA	EXAMPLE OF NEEDED EXPERTISE
*Engineering Competence	—To determine wasteload characteristics and processing needs.
	—To evaluate the initial and life cycle costs of alternative technical approaches.
	—To evaluate the operability of design alternatives.
	—To apply value engineering concepts.
*Construction Management and Cost Estimating Expertise	—To estimate construction costs. This should be done under alternatives of public versus private ownership.
*Public and Project Finance and Tax Expertise	—To estimate debt service costs under conventional financing approaches and privatization approaches.
	—To identify credit enhancement and risk reduction factors.
	—To evaluate alternative transaction structures in terms of tax benefits, cash flows, and user fees.
	—To test "what if" questions and perform sensitivity analyses of key data items.
	—To prepare project-specific financing plans.
*Legal Expertise	—To ensure that the transaction is structured in accordance with the applicable laws and regulations regarding the: • financial approach • procurement approach • operating approach • construction approach • covenants in existing agreements and debt issues
*Computer Simulation Expertise	—To create and utilize computer models to test resultant capital assessment, rate subsidy and operating fees, under alternative modes of financing and service provision.

Figure IX-1

private sector, in turn, has responsibilities to the public sector, which include the provision of a service with guarantees as to quality and cost.

When first approached with a privatization concept, public officials should possess a degree of healthy skepticism. All privatization proposals are not created equal. The private sector should be aware that privatization will not be well-received unless the public sector believes that the particular firm is qualified, trustworthy and willing to consider the community's interests along with its own. Flexibility on the part of both parties must be expected.

Privatization involves establishing a facility to deliver an on-going service, not a one-time sale. Relationships between the public and private sector must be more than that of buyer-seller. In a privatization transaction, there are a number of gates that both the public and private sectors must pass through together, including planning, negotiation, construction and long-term operation. The relationship should be established as a partnership. In the case of water supply and wastewater treatment, standards may change, facility expansion may be required, costs may change or other unforeseen events may occur after the facility has been put in service. Only in a spirit of partnership, flexibility and trust can these events be properly and equitably handled.

Working together to understand the other's needs and concerns, privatization partners can structure an approach through which risks are shared and needs are successfully met. Only through investments of time and effort will successful privatization partnerships be forged. The partnerships are well worth the effort, because, as has been shown by the pioneers of privatization, done right, both sides win.

Appendix A

PRIVATIZATION TAX ISSUES

Privatization has been described in this book as a public/private partnership. The underlying premise is that the arrangement provides each partner with benefits, but that neither party benefits at the expense of the other. This is well-illustrated by the tax benefits of a privatization transaction. Because the private sector can, in part, take advantage of tax benefits not available to tax-exempt municipalities, the net cost to the municipality of having the service provided can be lowered. Furthermore, the public sector can serve as a vehicle to provide tax-exempt financing, such as Industrial Development Bonds, resulting in lowered financing costs to the private sector. The benefits of lower project costs should be shared with those to be provided with the service in the form of lower user fees.

A discussion of the tax laws and related issues regarding privatization necessarily involves the use of terminology that may not be familiar to someone lacking a financial background. If such is the case, it is strongly recommended that the glossary at the end of this chapter be reviewed prior to reading the discussion which follows.

Historically, the federal government has provided significant incentives for investment in capital intensive projects through its tax laws. The benefits to business that came with passage of the Economic Recovery Tax Act of 1981 and The Tax Equity and Fiscal Responsibility Act of 1982 were heralded by many as the most significant in recent history. The key element of these acts, which provide the tax benefits of privatization transactions and all capital investments by qualifying taxpayers, is the establishment of a new depreciation system, the Accelerated Cost Recovery System (ACRS). Although the Deficit Reduction Act of 1984 has reduced some of the benefits provided by prior legislation, it has not significantly affected the attractiveness of privatization. In some areas, this legislation has provided guidelines that can be used to ensure the resultant economic viability of a project.

TAX BENEFITS

In privatization studies previously conducted, the present value of the economic benefits of ACRS depreciation and the Investment Tax Credit (ITC) alone have generally approximated 20% to 35% of the construction costs of a wastewater treatment facility. There are limits, however, on the ability of these tax benefits to affect a privatization transaction. First and foremost, the transaction must stand on its own economic merits, independent of the tax benefits. In other words, while the tax benefits of a privatization transaction may convert an ''attractive'' transaction into a ''very attractive'' one, any transaction that is not economically viable without the tax benefits should not be pursued. In such cases, the tax benefits may be disallowed by the Internal Revenue Service (IRS). However, through proper structuring of the service fees and the establishment of the residual value of the facility at the end of the financing period, the transaction may achieve ''economic merit''.

One of the most important tax benefits available to the private sector on a new facility is the ITC. The ITC is generally equal to 10% of the cost of personal property and other tangible property (but not including a building and its structural components), which is integrally related to the treatment process. ''Other tangible property,'' with respect to a wastewater treatment facility must meet the following test to qualify for the ITC: the structure can be expected to be replaced when the equipment it houses is replaced; and the structure cannot be economically used for another purpose. Generally, at least 80% to 90% of the cost of a typical wastewater treatment facility will qualify for the 10% ITC.

Normally, the ITC is claimed in the first year that a facility is in service. If, however, the construction period is greater than twenty-four months, the ITC can be claimed on a progress expenditure basis. The basis of property eligible for depreciation is reduced by one-half the ITC. To qualify for the ITC, the property must be new property, and cannot be owned, used, or leased by a municipality.

Property in a water or wastewater treatment facility not qualifying for the ITC would include land and any depreciable, real property not integrally related to the treatment process, such as an administration building. It is important to point out that while land does not qualify for the ITC, land improvements, including roads, excavation, concrete and/ or steel support for an in-ground tank or lagoon may qualify. The costs not qualifying for the ITC would typically be a relatively small portion of the total cost of a wastewater treatment facility.

There are limitations on the ITC. A taxpaying entity cannot claim an ITC greater than its tax liability. In most cases, the ITC is limited to 85% of the taxpayer's liability. The ITC is basically also subject to recapture rules. In other words, if property on which an investment credit has been claimed is sold, otherwise disposed of, or ceases to be qualifying property within five years after initially being placed in service, then all or a portion of the credit must be returned, depending on the length of the period of ownership. The owner's tax liability, or the amount owed to the government by the tax payer, is increased by a percentage of the investment tax credit previously allowed. If the property is disposed of, or ceases to be qualifying property within the first full year after being placed in service, the entire credit is recaptured. For each full year thereafter that the property is placed in service, the amount recaptured decreases by 20%. If, for example, the property is sold at the end of its third full year, 40% of the credit will be recaptured. If a property is sold in the sixth year after it is placed in service, none of the investment credit is recaptured.

An additional credit is generally available for certain energy related properties placed in service before December 31, 1985. Property eligibility is dependent upon there being a conversion of waste into a useful energy product. Energy property includes equipment for converting biomass into a synthetic solid, liquid or gaseous fuel. In a wastewater treatment plant, equipment for the capture of methane gas from sludge digestors would be an example of such property.

The energy credit is not available for public utility property (see below), or property that is owned, used or leased by a government unit. Similar to the reduction in the basis of property for five year depreciation due to the ITC, the basis is also reduced by half the energy tax credit. If a facility is financed by an Industrial Development Bond (IDB), the allowable business energy credit is reduced proportionately by the ratio of the portion financed to the cost of the property. For example, if 70%

of the cost of the property is financed by an IDB, only the remaining 30% of the cost is eligible for the energy credit. In addition, the energy credit is subject to recapture.

THE ACCELERATED COST RECOVERY SYSTEM

A major tax boost to encourage business investments came with the establishment of the Accelerated Cost Recovery System (ACRS) for depreciation of property. The type of property that qualifies for depreciation over five years by definition is the same property which qualifies for the investment tax credit: personal and certain other tangible property. Therefore, a significant portion of the assets related to a water or wastewater facility will qualify as five year recovery property (see discussion below for property financed with IDBs). The following percentages are used to depreciate five-year property:

Year	% of Asset Value Depreciated
1	15%
2	22
3	21
4	21
5	21

In utilizing the figures above, it is assumed that the owner has been engaged in the trade or business for the entire year. The depreciation is the same for the first year regardless of when during the year the property is placed in service, as long as the owner has been engaged in the trade or business for the entire year. If an owner commences his trade or business during the year of the acquisition of the property, then the depreciation in the first year must be prorated.

There are restrictions on ACRS depreciation of five-year property. Depreciation on five-year property is subject to recapture. This means that if the facility is sold at any time, any gain on five-year property will be taxed as ordinary income, to the extent of previous ACRS deductions claimed. Depreciation recapture, unlike ITC recapture, cannot be avoided by holding the property for a stipulated period of time. Any gain from the sale in excess of the original cost may be taxed as a capital gain, depending on the owner's individual circumstances.

To illustrate the concept of depreciation recapture, assume that qualified equipment with a basis of $100,000 was sold in the third year after it was placed in service. Based upon the previously mentioned ACRS percentages, the owner would be entitled to $15,000 and $22,000 worth of depreciation deductions in years 1 and 2, respectively. (No depreciation deduction is allowable for personal property in the year of disposition.) Consequently, the equipment would have an adjusted basis of $63,000 at the time of sale. If the equipment was sold for $90,000, the entire gain of $27,000 would be taxed at ordinary income rates, since it would be entirely attributable to the previously-deducted depreciation. Alternatively, if the equipment was sold for $125,000, $37,000 of that amount would be taxable as ordinary income and the remaining gain of $25,000 would be taxable at preferential capital gain rates.

Real property, such as buildings and structures, can be depreciated over a significantly shorter period using ACRS. (See discussion below for property financed with IDBs.) Generally, real property placed in service on or before March 15, 1984 can be depreciated under ACRS over as short as 15 years. For property placed in service after such date, the minimum recovery period is extended to 18 years. Under ACRS, 18 year real property is depreciated using the 175% declining balance method. However, the taxpayer may elect to use "straight line" depreciation over the same (18 year) period. Declining balance depreciation has the advantage of depreciating more of the property in the earlier years. However, when the declining balance method is used, any gain will first be attributable to the recapture of depreciation deductions and taxed as ordinary income; any remaining gain will be taxed at preferential capital gain rates. Consequently, the above example relating to personal property would also be illustrative of the characterization of the gain on the sale of real property if the declining method is used. (The only distinction is that a depreciation deduction would be allowable in the year of dispostion based on the number of months the property was in service in that year.) Alternatively, if the taxpayer elects to depreciate the property using the straight line method, there will be no recapture. Therefore, the entire gain will generally be taxed at preferential capital gain rates. However, in the case of corporations, twenty percent of all prior depreciation deductions would be treated as ordinary income.

If a privatization financing is accomplished through the issuance of IDBs, eligible depreciable property must be recovered using the straight line method of depreciation over the aforementioned applicable ACRS lives. Recently enacted legislation removed the previous exceptions from this provision for muncipal sewage or solid waste facilities and certain air or water pollution control facilities. Although such facilities can no longer be depreciated using ACRS, the ability to use the ACRS life (5 years for personal property and 18 years for real property) will still provide significantly greater economic benefits than those available prior to the enactment of ACRS.

A small portion of the cost of a water or wastewater treatment facility may not be depreciable. Any investment for land, even land purchased for a land-based facility, generally cannot be depreciated. However, expenditures made to improve land, including roads, excavations, concrete or steel support for inground tanks or lagoons, appear to qualify as five year ACRS property.

PUBLIC UTILITY PROPERTY

An issue that will affect the availablity of the tax benefits in a privatization transaction is whether or not the private sector firm will be treated as a public utility with regulated rates for tax purposes. Under IRS regulations, public utility property is eligible for ACRS, and therefore is depreciated under the same guidelines as a non-regulated company, if the taxpayer uses a normalization method of accounting. In brief, the normalization method requires that a utility calculate its tax expense for rate making purposes using the same depreciation method and at least as long a depreciation period as it uses to compute its depreciation for its financial statements. However, regulatory bodies in many states do not allow utilities to normalize the tax benefits of ACRS. Accordingly, due care is essential in structuring the transaction to ensure that the anticipated tax benefits are realized.

It is likely that most privatization transactions will be structured so that the private sector firm, as a wholesaler, will charge the municipality or authority for the treatment service. It would then be up to the municipality to charge the individual users on a retail basis. Using this approach, the private sector firm will most likely not be considered a public utility. However, state laws must be investigated by qualified counsel. For tax purposes, public utility property is defined as property used by a taxpayer predominantly in connection with the furnishing or selling of electrical energy, water or sewage disposal services, gas or steam via a pipeline, etc., when the rates for the company's goods and services have been establised or approved by a state or political subdivision, commission or agency of the United States.

Regulations specify that public utility property exists only where rates are regulated on a rate-of-return basis, such that the revenues cover a taxpayer's cost of providing the service, and include a fair return on the taxpayer's investment in the facility. If a schedule of rates is filed with a regulatory body that has the authority to approve such rates on that basis, the rates are regulated even if the regulatory body takes no action on the filed schedule. For these reasons, attention must be given to understanding the consequences of public utility property designation for tax purposes.

PRIVATIZATION: USERS OF THE TAX BENEFITS

Many people believe that privatization transactions will not lend themselves to "typical, individual, tax shelter investors," because of provisions in the tax laws called the "at risk rules." The "at risk rules" prohibit individuals or closely held corporations from claiming losses and investment credits on costs in excess of the amount for which the investor is at risk. Therefore, unless the investor is personally liable for the financing, termed "recourse financing," he will not be able to claim deductions in excess of the actual capital he has contributed. Because it is anticipated that most of the financing packages for privatization transactions will be non-recourse financing, individuals, closely-held corporations and personal holding companies will not necessarily be interested in investing in these transactions. As a result, many believe that the initial market for owners and investors in privatized facilities will be those who have a vested interest in seeing the water and wastewater industry prosper, such as construction firms, consulting engineers, equipment manufacturing firms and equipment leasing companies. However, as the privatization concept for wastewater facilities becomes more widely accepted, it is possible that transactions will be structured with sufficient credit enhancements and protection, so that on an "at risk basis," individual and corporate investors will seek to participate.

SERVICE CONTRACT ARRANGEMENTS

Because of the restrictions on the availability of the ITC and ACRS lives and methods where there is deemed to be a municipal user of the property, the use of a service contract permits the maximum utilization of tax benefits associated with the construction of a facility. Presently, there exists only limited statutory and judicial guidance which can be used to properly structure a service contract.

However, under the 1984 tax legislation, six criteria have been provided for determining whether a valid service contract exists, or if, conversely, the arrangement more nearly resembles a lease:

1. Physical possession of the property by a tax-exempt entity would be indicative of a lease.

2. If the service recipient (a tax-exempt entity) has the right to dictate the manner in which the property is operated, maintained or improved, it would be a characteristic of a lease.

3. A contract that conveys significant possessory or economic interest in the property by the service recipient resembles a lease. Factors that will be considered include whether the recipient bears any risk if the property declines in value or would share in any appreciation if the property appreciates in value.

4. The service provider should bear the risk of substantially diminished receipts or substantially increased expenditures if a valid service contract exists.

5. If the property is concurrently used to provide services to others who are unrelated to the tax-exempt entity, it would be indicative of a service contract.

6. If the total contract price substantially exceeds the rental value of the property, it would be indicative of a valid service contract. If the contract separately charges for services and for use of the property, it would be characteristic of a lease.

Overall, the determination of whether an arrangement is a valid service contract or a lease will be dependent upon all relevant facts, including the six points listed above. However, if a particular factor is irrelevant to a specific case, it should not affect the final determination.

Exempt from the rules cited above are the following:

- Qualified solid waste disposal facilities;
- Certain cogeneration facilities;
- Water treatment facilities.

However, service contract arrangements for such facilities will be treated as leases if the tax-exempt entity (or a related entity):

- Operates the facility.
- Bears any significant financial burden for nonperformance under the contract for reasons other than those beyond the control of the service provider.
- Receives any financial benefit as a result of technological changes which improve efficiencies and reduce costs; or
- Has an option to purchase, or may be required to purchase, all or part of the facility at a fixed or determinable price, other than at fair market value.

In addition, in *Xerox Corporation vs. United States* 656 f2d 659 (1981), the Supreme Court has also provided some guidance in the area of service contracts. In this case, Xerox claimed that its arrangements with customers, including agencies of the U.S. government, were service contracts, and the U.S. argued they were leases. The case was decided in favor of Xerox, based on criteria which included the following:

- The taxpayer (Xerox) retained control of the machines.
- Xerox bore the risk of loss.
- Xerox had the right to remove and replace the machines with similar machines offering similar capacity.
- Xerox was responsible for making all the repairs.
- The machines were an integral part of providing the service.
- Customer payment was based on usage, not on the duration of the service.

These criteria should be given appropriate consideration in structuring privatization transactions.

For privatization transactions, a service contract approach rather than a traditional leasing arrangement is preferred. If property is leased to and thereby used by a tax-exempt entity, it is ineligible for ITC and cannot be depreciated using ACRS. Under the recent tax legislation, if personal property, which is otherwise 5 year ACRS property, is used by a tax-exempt entity, it must be depreciated using the straight line method over 12 years (or present class life) or 125% of the lease term, whichever is greater. For real property (18 year ACRS property) depreciation is allowed using the straight line method over the greater of 40 years (or present class life) or 125% of the lease term. There are additional rules concerning the leasing of real property which are beyond the scope of this appendix but should be addressed if a leasing arrangement is being considered.

RESIDUAL VALUE

It may be appropriate for a privatized facility to be privately owned for only a finite period of time, because either the investors may want to own the facility only during the period of greatest after-tax cash flow, or because it may be politically desirable that the municipality have the option to eventually take over the facility at a future date. There are risks associated with this idea for both the public and private sectors. If the municipality wants to have the right to own the facility, it may ask to have that stipulated in the contract between itself and the private sector firm. If a purchase price is not written into the contract, a municipality runs the risk of paying fair market value for the facility at a future date. If a nominal purchase price is quoted in the contract, the private concern is taking a risk that the IRS will disallow the tax benefits to the private firm. This disallowance will occur if the IRS determines that the entire transaction is simply a sophisticated way for the private sector to lend money to the public sector.

There is much concern with respect to what can and should happen with a facility when the financing has been repaid. Some political officials have the idea that the private sector firm will merely turn over the facility to the public sector at the end of the financing period. In all likelihood, a transaction structured in this manner will not generate the desired tax benefits, since the private sector does not retain ownership and no ownership transfer mechanism has been included in the transaction. A contract between a municipality and the private sector must have a provision for the private sector to remain the real, beneficial owner during the period of ownership. If a contract has a mechanism by which the municipality can acquire ownership of the facility when the financing period comes to an end, that option must be tied to the fair market value of the facility at the time of purchase. As discussed above, this mechanism is related to the question of residual value.

At the time of this writing, there are limited IRS rulings on privatization transactions, and a general lack of definitive guidance on the acceptable mechanism for transferring the ownership of a privatized facility. There are, however, rulings on leasing arrangements which can be used for guidance. These rules require that, in order to obtain an advance ruling from the Service that the transaction constitutes a true lease, any purchase option given the lessee should be at fair market value determined at the time the option is exercised. However, case law does exist which indicates that under certain circumstances, purchase options at other than fair market value will not necessarily invalidate a lease. Until the recently enacted Deficit Reduction Act of 1984, there were no statutory or judicial guidelines for determining the IRS treatment of a service contract with a non-fair market value option. It was therefore reasonable to assume that the lease guidelines could be extrapolated to deal with service contracts.

As discussed earlier, the provisions of the Deficit Reduction Act of 1984 detail six criteria for determining whether a valid service contract exists. These criteria do not include any requirements regarding a purchase option; however, as noted earlier, service contracts for certain facilities (which include solid waste disposal, cogeneration and water treatment facilities) are excepted from the general service contract criteria only if, among other requirements, they do not contain a non-fair market value purchase option.

Consequently, a privatization transaction involving a wastewater treatment facility which includes a fair market value option should ordinarily be considered a service contract. On the other hand, a transaction with other than a fair market value option may still qualify as a service contract, but will be required to run a far more complicated and subjective gauntlet of tests to do so. In either case, the entire arrangement should be structured so that the parties can demonstrate that the arrangement is not in reality a means of simply providing a financing mechanism to the public sector, but rather that the risks and rewards of the ownership of the facility, including the residual value risk, rest with the private sector.

How a municipality finances the exercise of its repurchase option should be left up to the municipality and its financial advisors. However, one alternative is for the municipality to retail the service at a price in excess of the price at which the service is available wholesale. The additional monies can be placed in a fund dedicated to financing the buy-back option. Three or four variations of this theme exist, as well as certain alternative approaches, to enable the public sector to take ownership of a facility in a financially non-disruptive manner. The approach that is finally selected must be tied to site and project specific circumstances. In addition, the private sector must understand that, the greater the degree of involvement on its part in providing funds for the municipality to buy a facility, the greater the risk that the IRS will challenge the tax benefits. This, however, should not preclude the private sector firm and its advisors from suggesting possible alternatives.

While the privatization approach is not in itself complex, the tax issues are somewhat difficult to interpret and many are interrelated. Structuring of a privatization transaction should not be undertaken without the advice and guidance of qualified individuals, including advisors knowledgeable in taxation.

GLOSSARY OF TAX TERMS

Accelerated Cost Recovery System (ACRS): The ACRS establishes useful lives for most depreciable property placed in service after 1980 for the purpose of recovering a property's capital cost. This system establishes recovery periods of 3, 5, 10, 15 and 18 years, and various methods of accelerated depreciation depending on the type of property.

Asset: Property, both tangible and intangible, which belongs to an individual or corporation.

Basis: The actual cost of a property to the taxpayer. It is used to determine depreciation, gain or loss on the sale of a property for tax purposes.

Capital Gain: Gain from the sale of certain assets, principally those other than inventory, accounts receivable and depreciable assets, which is subject to a special reduced tax rate.

Closely-Held Corporation: For purposes of the "at risk rules," a corporation in which five or fewer individuals own more than 50% of the corporation.

Depreciation: A reduction in the value of an asset due to use or obsolescence. For tax purposes, depreciation is the deduction from taxable income of the cost of a tangible asset over its estimated life, or over a statutory recovery period. See Accelerated Cost Recovery System.

Equity: Capital that has been, or is obligated to be, contributed by the project owner.

Fair Market Value: The price that would be paid for a property if it was offered for sale in a competitive market where both buyer and seller have complete information, and neither is under any compulsion to buy or sell.

Fair Market Value Purchase Option: An option to purchase leased property from the lessor at the end of the lease term for the property's fair market value.

Fixed Price Purchase Option: The option to purchase an asset at the conclusion of the lease term or service contract, for a pre-agreed purchase price.

Industrial Development Bonds (IDBs):   Bonds, issued by a government or government development agency, the proceeds of which are used to build business facilities which are usually used by a private business.

Investment Tax Credit (ITC):   The ITC is a direct tax credit, calculated as a percentage of the qualified cost of certain depreciable property.

Lease: A contract for which the lessor turns over the right of possession and use of a property to the lessee in exchange for periodic payment over a specified time period.

Personal Property: Generally, all assets other than real property, or any rights or interests in real property.

Public Utility Property: Property used primarily to furnish a service such as electrical energy, water, gas or steam (via a pipeline), or sewage disposal services at a rate which has been approved by a governmental entity or agency, based on a rate of return on investment basis.

Real Property: Immovable property (i.e., land) and that which grows or is built on it.

Recapture: Recovery of previously received tax benefits. In the case of depreciation, at the time of the sale of an asset, the owner's gain is treated as ordinary income, rather than as capital gain, to the extent of depreciation claimed. Under certain circumstances, all or part of the previously claimed investment tax credit must be added to the taxpayer's tax liability.

Recourse Financing: A method of financing in which the investor is held personally responsible for payment of the debt.

Residual Value: The fair market value of an asset at the end of the lease term expressed in present dollars.

Service Contract: An agreement between two parties that one performs a service for the other for a specified time period at a specified cost.

Tangible Property: All property which is a physical object.

Appendix B

UTAH PRIVATIZATION ACT
1984
SECOND SPECIAL SESSION

Enrolled Copy
S. B. No. 1   By Fred W. Finlinson

AN ACT RELATING TO THE PRIVATIZATION OF CITY AND COUNTY CAPITAL
PROJECTS; GIVING AUTHORITY TO CITIES AND COUNTIES TO ENTER INTO
LONG-TERM SERVICE CONTRACTS WITH PRIVATE OWNER/OPERATORS OF
DRINKING WATER, WATER, AND WASTEWATER FACILITIES; AUTHOR-
IZING THE ISSUANCE OF INDUSTRIAL DEVELOPMENT BONDS TO FINANCE
THE ACQUISITION OR CONSTRUCTION OF THOSE FACILITIES; AND PRO-
VIDING AN EFFECTIVE DATE.

THIS ACT ENACTS CHAPTER 10d, TITLE 73, UTAH CODE ANNOTATED 1953.

Be it enacted by the Legislature of the State of Utah:

Section 1. Chapter 10d, Title 73, Utah Code Annotated 1953, is
enacted to read:

73-10d-1. *The legislature declares that the policy of this state is
to assure its citizens adequate public services, including drinking water,
water, and wastewater collection treatment and disposal at reasonable
cost. Adequate public services are essential to the maintenance and general welfare of the citizens of this state and to the continued expansion
of the state's economy, job market, and industrial base.*

*The cost of constructing, owning, and operating capital facilities to
meet the anticipated growth in the demand for those public services is
becoming increasingly burdensome to cities and counties, particularly
to the smaller communities of the state.*

It is desirable that innovative financing mechanisms be made available to assist the communities of this state to develop capital facilities to provide adequate public services at reasonable cost. Private sector ownership and operation of capital facilities providing public services together with industrial development revenue bond financing of those facilities, can result in cost savings to communities contracting for those public services.

It is in the best public interest of the state and its citizens that cities and counties be authorized to provide public services by financing capital projects owned and operated by private persons through the issuance of industrial development revenue bonds, and to contract with private persons for the long-term provision of the services of those facilities.

73-10d-2.   *This act shall be known and may be cited as the "Utah Privatization Act."*

73-10d-3.   *As used in this chapter:*

(1) "Bonds" means industrial development revenue bonds, including umbrella bonds, notes, or other obligations issued by a city or county.

(2) "Cost" means the cost of acquiring, constructing, and financing any privatization project and placing the privatization project in service, including, without limitation: the cost of acquisition and construction of any facility or any modification, improvement, or extension of that facility; any cost incident to the acquisition of any necessary property, easement, or right-of-way; engineering or architectural fees, legal fees, and fiscal agents' and financial advisors' fees; any cost incurred for any preliminary planning to determine the economic and engineering feasibility of a proposed privatization project; and costs of economic investigations and studies, surveys, preparation of designs, plans, working drawings, specifications, and the inspection and supervision of the construction of any facility and any other cost incurred by the city or county.

(3) "Drinking water project" means any work or facility necessary or desirable to provide water for human consumption and other domestic uses which has at least 15 service connections or serves an average of 25 individuals daily for at least 60 days of the year and includes collection, treatment, storage, and distribution facilities under the control of the operator and used primarily with the system, and collection, pretreatment, or storage facilities used primarily in connection with the

*system but not under such control, and any related structures and fa-
cilities.*

*(4) "Facility" means any structure, building, machinery, system,
land, water right, or other property necessary or desirable to provide
the services contemplated by a privatization project, including, without
limitation, all related and appurtenant easements and rights-of-way, improvements, utilities, landscaping, sidewalks, roads, curbs and gutters,
and equipment and furnishings.*

*(5) "Governing body" means the body in which the legislative pow-
ers of the city or county are vested.*

*(6) "Long-term agreement" means an agreement or contract having
a term of more than five years and less than 50 years.*

*(7) "Private owner/operator" means a person that is not a public
entity and which owns and operates a privatization project.*

*(8) "Privatization project" means any drinking water, water, or
wastewater project which is owned or operated by a private person, and
provides the related services to public entities. This includes, but is not
limited to:*

*(a) the acquisition, construction, reconstruction, repair, alter-
ation, modernization, renovation, improvement, or extension of any such
project, whether or not in existence or under construction, and the financing of those activities;*

*(b) the purchase, installation, or financing of equipment, ma-
chinery, and other personal property required by such project; or*

*(c) the acquisition, improvement, or financing of real estate and
the extension or provision of utilities, access roads, and other appurtenant facilities, all of which are to be used or occupied by any person in
providing drinking water, water, and wastewater services.*

*(9) "Public entity" means the state, a city, a county, or other po-
litical subdivision, agency, or instrumentality.*

*(10) "Short-term agreement" means any contract or agreement having
a term less than five years.*

*(11) "Supervising agency" means the Water Development Coordi-
nating Council created in Section 73-10c-3.*

*(12) "Wastewater project" means any sewer, sewer system, sewage
treatment facility and system, lagoon, sewage collection facility and system and related pipelines, and all similar systems, works, and facilities*

necessary or desirable to collect, hold, cleanse, or purify any sewage or other polluted waters of this state, and related structures and facilities.

(13) "Water project" means any work or facility necessary or desirable to conserve, develop, protect, or treat the waters of this state including, without limitation, any reservoir, diversion dam, electrical generation system, irrigation dam and system, culinary water system, water work, water treatment facility, canal, ditch, aqueduct, pipeline, and related structures and facilities.

73-10d-4. *The governing body of the public entity considering entering into a privatization project agreement shall issue a notice of intention setting forth a summary of the agreement provisions and the time within which and place at which petitions may be filed requesting the calling of an election in the area affected by the agreement to determine whether the agreement should be approved. The notice of intention shall specify the form of the petitions. If, within 30 days after the publication of the notice of intention, a petition is filed with the governing body of the public entity by at least 5% of the qualified electors of the area (as certified by the county clerks of the respective counties comprising the area) requesting an election be held to authorize the agreement, the governing body shall proceed to call and hold an election. If an adequate petition is not filed within 30 days, the governing body may adopt a resolution so finding and may proceed to enter into the agreement. Then, subject to the powers and rules of the supervising agency, the governing body of each public entity may:*

(1) supervise and regulate the construction, maintenance, ownership, and operation of all privatization projects within its jurisdiction;

(2) contract, by entry into short- or long-term agreements with private owner/operators for the provision within its jurisdiction of the services of privatization projects;

(3) levy and collect taxes, fees, and charges as appropriate, and pledge, assign, or otherwise convey as security for the payment of its bonds any revenues and receipts derived from such fees or charges;

(4) require licenses as appropriate to discharge its responsibility to supervise and regulate the construction, maintenance, ownership, and operation of a privatization project.

(5) control the right to contract, maintain, own, and operate all

drinking water, water, and wastewater projects and the services provided in connection with such projects within its jurisdiction;

(6) agree that the sole and exclusive right to provide the services within its jurisdiction related to privatization projects be assumed by any private owner/operator;

(7) contract for the lease or purchase of land, facilities, equipment, and vehicles for the operation of privatization projects;

(8) convey land, facilities, equipment, and vehicles, whether or not previously used in connection with privatization projects, to private owner/operators;

(9) establish policies for the operation of any privatization project within its jurisdiction, including hours of operation, the character and kinds of services, and other rules necessary for the safety of operating personnel; and

(10) issue industrial development revenue bonds under Chapter 17, Title 11, Utah Industrial Facilities Development Act, to finance the costs of privatization projects located within its jurisdiction, on behalf of public entities that constitute the users of the services provided by those projects, which projects shall provide the services of drinking water, water, and wastewater projects to one or more public or private entities, all pursuant to contracts and other arrangements provided for in the proceedings under which the bonds are issued.

73-10d-5. *(1) Bonds issued under this chapter do not constitute a debt or liability of this state or of any county or city, or any other political subdivision of the state. Those bonds do not constitute the loaning of the credit of the state or of any county or city, or any other political subdivision of the state. The bonds are not payable from funds other than those of the city or county specifically set aside for such purpose. All of the bonds shall contain on the face a statement to the effect: (a) that the governing body is obligated to pay them solely from the revenues of the privatization project; (b) that neither the state nor any political subdivision of the state is obligated to pay the bonds; and (c) that neither the faith and credit nor the taxing power of the state or any political subdivision of the state is pledged to the payment of principal, premium, or the interest on those bonds.*

(2) All expenses incurred in carrying out this chapter are payable solely as provided under this chapter, and nothing in this chapter may

be construed to authorize the governing body to incur indebtedness or liability on behalf of or payable by the state or any political subdivision of the state.

(3) Any short- or long-term agreement entered into between a public entity and a private owner/operator for the provision of the services of a privatization project are considered an exercise of that public entity's business or proprietary power binding upon its succeeding governing bodies. Any payments made by a public entity for services received under a short- or long-term agreement with a private owner/operator may not be construed to be an indebtedness or a lending of credit of the public entity within the meaning of any constitutional or statutory restriction.

(4) A privatization project or its private owner/operator is not deemed a "public utility" as defined in Section 54-2-1.

(5) For purposes of Chapter 17, Title 11, Utah Industrial Facilities Development Act, a privatization project is deemed a financeable "project" as defined in Subsection 11-17-2 (2).

73-10d-6. *(1) If a public entity issues bonds to finance the cost of a privatization project and the bonds mature more than ten years after the bonded project begins operation, the public entity contracting with a private owner/operator for the services of the privatization project shall assure that the minimum level of services under contract, payment for the services and the supply of drinking water, water, and wastewater required in connection with the provision of those services will be sufficient to generate enough income, after payment of operating expenses, reserves for repair and replacement, and to discharge any other obligation of the public entity to the private owner/operator under any short- or long-term agreement, together with all other sources of revenue pledged for payment of the bonds, to pay all principal and interest on the bonds during the term of the bonded indebtedness. The assurance may take the form of:*

(a) long-term agreements (at least equal to the period of the bonded indebtedness) with other public entities or other persons; or

(b) ordinances, franchises, or other forms of regulation requiring sufficient quantities of drinking water, water, and wastewater.

(2) The supervising agency shall establish rules for periodic reporting by any public entity that establishes ordinances, franchises, or other forms of regulation under Subsection (1) and Subsection

73-10d-4 (1). The reports shall include information about the services being provided by the privatization project and whether the charges made for those services together with all other sources of revenue pledged for the payment of principal and interest on the bonds, are sufficient to meet the debt service on the bonds.

73-10d-7. *(1) Any one or more public entities, or the United States or its agencies, may enter into long-term agreements with any person for joint or cooperative action related to the acquisition, construction, maintenance, ownership, operation, and improvement of a privatization project pursuant to which the services of privatization projects are made available in accordance with the terms, conditions, and consideration provided in the agreement. Any payments made by a public entity for services received under the agreement may not be construed to be an indebtedness of the public entity within the meaning of any constitutional or statutory restriction, and no election is necessary for the authorization of the agreement.*

(2) Any one or more public entities together with any private entity may construct or otherwise acquire joint interests in any privatization project or any part of a privatization project, for their common use, or may sell to any other public entity or person a partial interest in a privatization project. Any public entity otherwise qualifying under Chapter 17, Title 11, Utah Industrial Facilities Development Act, may issue its bonds under this chapter for the purpose of acquiring a joint interest in a project, or any part of a project, whether the joint interest is to be acquired through construction of a new project or the purchase of an interest in an existing project.

Section 2. This act shall take effect upon approval by the governor on the day following the constitutional time limit of Article VII, Sec. 8 without the governor's signature, or in the case of veto, the date of veto override.

Appendix C

NEW JERSEY WASTEWATER TREATMENT PRIVATIZATION ACT
(Passage Pending)

5/15/84-R-47
5/16/84, 5/17/84

Senate Committee Substitute
for S-991

AN ACT concerning long-term contracts between local government units and private firms for the provision of wastewater treatment services, establishing a procedure for the negotiating, awarding, and review of these contracts, amending P.L. 1971, c. 198, and supplementing Title 58 of the Revised Statutes. BE IT ENACTED by the Senate and General Assembly of the State of New Jersey:

1. This act shall be known and may be cited as the "New Jersey Wastewater Treatment Privatization Act."

2. The Legislation finds and declares that protecting the ground and surface water of the state from pollution is vital to the health and general welfare of the citizens of New Jersey; that the construction, rehabilitation, operation, and maintenance of modern and efficient sewer systems and wastewater treatment plants are essential to protecting and improving the state's water quality; that in addition to protecting and improving water quality, adequate wastewater treatment systems are essential to economic growth and development; that many of the wastewater treatment systems in New Jersey must be replaced or upgraded if an inexorable decline in water quality is to be avoided during the coming decades; that the United States Congress, in recognition of the crucial role wastewater treatment systems and plants play in maintaining and improving water quality, and with an understanding that the cost of financing and constructing these systems must be borne by local governments and authorities with limited sources of revenues, established in the "Clean Water Act" a program to provide local governments with grants for constructing these systems; that during the last several years the amount of federal grant money available to states and local governments for assistance in constructing and improving wastewater treatment systems has sharply diminished; that the current level of federal grant funding is inadequate to meet the cost of upgrading the state's wastewater treatment capacity to comply with state water quality standards; that given this inadequate present level of federal grant funding, alternative methods of financing the construction, operation, and improvement of wastewater treatment systems must be developed and encouraged; that one alternative method of financing necessary wastewater treatment systems available to local government units consists of contracting with private-sector firms for the financing, construction and operation of these systems; and that for some local government units, contracting for the provision of wastewater treatment services, if done in such a way as to protect the interests of consumers and to conform with environmental standards, will constitute an appropriate method of securing these needed wastewater treatment systems.

The Legislature therefore determines that it is in the public interest to establish a comprehensive procedure designed to authorize local government units to contract with private firms for the provision of wastewater treatment services.

3. As used in this act:

a. "Contracting unit" means a county, municipality, municipal or county sewerage or utility authority, municipal sewerage district, joint meeting or any other political subdivision of the state authorized pursuant to law to construct wastewater treatment systems or provide wastewater treatment services.

b. "Department" means the Department of Environmental Protection.

c. "Division" means the Division of Local Government Services in the Department of Community Affairs.

d. "Vendor" means any person financially, technically, and administratively capable of financing, planning, designing, constructing, operating, or maintaining, or any combination thereof, a wastewater treatment system, or of providing wastewater treatment services to a local government unit under the terms of a contract awarded pursuant to the provisions of this act.

e. "Wastewater" means residential, commercial, industrial, or agricultural liquid waste, sewerage, stormwater runoff, or any combination thereof, or other liquid residue discharged or collected into a sewer system or stormwater system, or any combination thereof.

f. "Wastewater treatment system" means any equipment, plants, structures, machinery, apparatus, or land, or any combination thereof, acquired, used, constructed or operated for the storage, collection, reduction, recycling, reclamation, disposal, separation, or other treatment of wastewater or sewer sludge, or for the final disposal of residues resulting from the treatment of wastewater, including, but not limited to, pumping and ventilating stations, facilities, plants and works, connections, outfall sewers, interceptors, trunk lines, and other personal property and appurtenances necessary for their use or operation.

g. "Wastewater treatment services" means services provided by a wastewater treatment system.

4. The provisions of any other law, or rules and regulations adopted pursuant thereto to the contrary notwithstanding, any contracting unit may enter into a contract with a vendor for the financing, designing, construction, operation, or maintenance, or any combination thereof, of a wastewater treatment system, or for wastewater treatment services, pursuant to the provisions of this act.

5. A contracting unit which intends to enter into a contract with a private vendor for the provision of wastewater treatment services pursuant to the provisions of this act shall notify, at least 60 days prior to issuing a request for qualifications from interested vendors pursuant to section 6 of this act, the division, the department, and the Department of the Public Advocate of its intention, and shall publish notice of its intention in at least one newspaper of general circulation in the jurisdiction which would be served under the terms of the proposed contract.

6. Upon submitting the notices of intent pursuant to section 5 of this act, a contracting unit may issue a request for qualifications of vendors interested in entering into a contract with the contracting unit for the provision of wastewater treatment services. The request for qualifications shall include a general description of the wastewater treatment services required by the contracting unit, the minimum acceptable qualifications to be possessed by a vendor proposing to enter into a contract for the provisions of these services, and the date by which vendors must submit their qualifications. In addition to all other factors bearing on qualification, the contracting unit shall consider the reputation and experience of the vendor, and may consider information which might result in debarment or suspension of a vendor from State contracting and may disqualify a vendor if the vendor has been debarred or suspended by a State agency. The request for qualifications shall be published in at least one appropriate professional or trade journal, and in at least one newspaper of general circulation in the jurisdiction which would be served under the terms of the proposed contract.

7. After reviewing the qualifications submitted by vendors pursuant to section 6 of this act, a contracting unit shall establish a list of all vendors responding to the request for qualifications, and shall designate the vendor or vendors which the contracting unit has determined to be qualified to provide the wastewater treatment services described in the request for qualifications. This list shall include a statement setting forth the criteria applied by the contracting unit in selecting qualified vendors, and shall be published in the same publications in which the requests for qualifications were published pursuant to section 6 of this act.

8. Upon selecting the qualified vendors pursuant to section 7 of this act, a contracting unit shall transmit a request for proposals to the qualified vendors, which shall include a detailed description of the wastewater treatment system and services required, the format and procedure to be followed in submitting proposals, the specific information which the vendor must provide in the proposal, a statement setting forth the relative importance of factors, including cost, which the contracting unit will consider in evaluating a proposal submitted by a qualified vendor, and any other information which the contracting unit deems appropriate. The request for proposals shall include the date and time of day by which, and the place at which, the proposals shall be submitted to the contracting unit. The contracting unit may extend the deadline for submission of proposals, but this extension shall apply to all qualified vendors, who shall be provided with simultaneous written notification of this extension.

9. A contracting unit shall review proposals submitted by vendors

pursuant to section 8 of this act in such a manner as to avoid disclosure of the contents of any proposal to vendors submitting competing proposals. If provided for in the request for proposals, the contracting unit may conduct discussions with qualified vendors who have submitted proposals for the purpose of clarifying any information submitted in the proposal, or assuring that the vendor fully understood and responded to the requirements set forth in the request for proposals. If, as as result of these discussions, the contracting unit decides to revise the request for proposals, it shall immediately notify in writing each qualified vendor which has submitted a proposal of any such revision or revisions to the request for proposals. In the event of any revision in the requests for proposals, a qualified vendor shall be permitted to submit revisions to its proposal.

10. After reviewing the proposals submitted by qualified vendors pursuant to section 9 of this act, a contracting unit shall designate in writing the selected vendor or vendors. This designation shall include a list of the qualified vendors submitting proposals, the basis on which the selected vendor or vendors was chosen, and a finding that the proposal submitted by the selected vendor or vendors constitutes the proposal most advantageous to the jurisdiction to be served under the terms of the proposal, based upon the evaluation factors included in the request for proposals. This designation shall be published in at least one newspaper in general circulation in the jurisdiction to be served under the terms of the proposal.

11. Upon designating the selected vendor or vendors pursuant to section 10 of this act, a contracting unit shall negotiate with the selected vendor or vendors a proposed contract, which shall include the accepted proposal and the provisions required pursuant to section 15 of this act. Upon negotiating a proposed contract, the contracting unit shall make the proposed contract available to the public at its main offices, and shall transmit a copy of the proposed contract to the division, the department, and the Department of the Public Advocate.

12. a. A contracting unit shall conduct a public hearing or hearings on the charges, rates, or fees, or the formula for determining these charges, rates, or fees, and the other provisions contained in a proposed contract negotiated pursuant to section 11 of this act. The contracting unit shall provide at least 90 days public notice of this public hearing to the Department of the Public Advocate, prospective consumers, and other interested parties. This notice shall be published in at least one newspaper of general circulation in the jurisdiction to be served under the terms of the proposed contract. Within 45 days after giving notice of the public hearing, the contracting unit shall hold a meeting with prospective consumers and other interested parties to explain the terms and conditions of the proposed contract, and to receive written questions which will be part of the record of the public hearing. At the public hearing, the selected vendor or vendors shall be present, and the contracting unit shall have the burden to answer the questions received at the meeting, and to show that the proposed contract complies with the provisions of section 15 of this act, and that it constitutes the best means of securing the required wastewater treatment services among available alternatives. The contracting unit shall provide that a verbatim record be kept of the public hearing, and that a written transcript of this record be printed and made available to the public within 30 days of the close of the public hearing. After the public hearing the contracting unit and the vendor may agree to make changes to the proposed contract, and shall transmit the proposed contract, a copy of the printed transcript of the public hearing, and a statement summarizing the major issues raised at the public hearing and the response of the contracting unit to these issues, to the division, the department, and the Department of the Public Advocate, and to all persons who attended the public hearing.

b. If the Division of Rate Counsel in the Department of the Public Advocate represents the public interest at a public hearing or hearings conducted pursuant to this section, the Division of Rate Counsel shall be entitled to assess the vendor for costs incurred in this representation in the manner provided in section 20 of P.L. 1974, c. 27 (C.52:27E-19). The basis of the assessment shall be the prospective first year's revenue realized by the vendor from the provision of the wastewater treatment services pursuant to the terms of the proposed contract.

c. If a contract awarded pursuant to the provisions of this act is renegotiated, the contracting unit shall conduct a public hearing on the renegotiated contract pursuant to the provisions of this section.

13. a. The department, within 60 days of receipt of a proposed contract submitted to it by a contracting unit pursuant to section 12 of this act, shall approve or conditionally approve the proposed contract. If the department approves the proposed contract, it shall accompany its approval with a written finding that the proposed contract will meet appropriate environmental and water quality standards, and that it is consistent with the areawide and facility water quality management plans adopted for the jurisdiction to be served under the terms of the proposed contract pursuant to the "Water Quality Planning Act," P.L. 1977, c. 75 (C.58:11A-1 et seq.). If the department conditionally approves a proposed contract, it shall state in writing the revisions which must be made to the proposed contract prior to receiving approval, and shall inform the contracting units if the revisions to be made to the proposed contract warrant a public hearing. After revising the contract, the contracting unit may resubmit the proposed contract to the department for approval.

   b. The division, within 60 days of receipt of a proposed contract transmitted to it by a contracting unit pursuant to section 12 of this act, shall approve or conditionally approve the proposed contract. If the division approves the proposed contract, it shall accompany its approval with a written finding that the proposed contract complies with the provisions of section 15 of this act, and that the proposed contract is compatible with the fiscal and financial capabilities of the contracting unit. If the division conditionally approves the proposed contract, it shall state in writing the revisions which must be made to the proposed contract prior to receiving approval, and shall inform the contracting unit if the revisions to be made to the proposed contract warrant a public hearing. After revising the proposed contract, the contracting unit may resubmit the proposed contract to the division for approval.

   14. a. A contracting unit may award a contract negotiated pursuant to the provisions of this act to a vendor only after the department and the division have approved the proposed contract pursuant to section 13 of this act.

   15. Any contract for the provision of wastewater treatment services negotiated and awarded to a vendor by a contracting unit pursuant to [this act], or the "Local Public Contracts Law," P.L. 1971 , c. 198 (C.40A:11-1 et seq.), shall include, but shall not be limited to, provisions concerning:

   a. The allocation of the risks of financing and constructing a wastewater treatment system, including delays in completion of the construction of the system, construction and financing cost overruns and increased costs resulting from change orders, construction changes required by revisions in applicable laws, rules, or regulations, failure of the system to achieve its required operating performance or efficiency, changes in tax benefits, and the need for equity contributions in addition to those provided for in the contract;

b. The allocation of the risks of operating and maintaining a wastewater treatment system, including excessive or non-scheduled periods of inoperation or technical failure, excess labor and materials costs due to underestimation, changes in operating procedures required by revisions in applicable law, rules, or regulations, changes in the quantity or composition of wastewater delivered for treatment, excessive operation or maintenance costs due to poor management, and increased costs of disposal of the residue resulting from wastewater treatment;

c. The allocation of the risks associated with circumstances or occurrences beyond the control of the parties to the contract;

d. The defaulting and termination of the contract;

e. The periodic preparation by the vendor of an operating performance report and an audited balance statement of the wastewater treatment system, which shall be submitted to the contracting unit, the department and the division;

f. The intervals at which the contract shall be renegotiated;

g. The employment of current employees of the contracting unit whose positions or employment will be affected by the terms of the contract; and

h. The formulas to be used to determine the charges, rates, or fees to be charged for the wastewater treatment services, and the methodology or methodologies used to develop these formulas.

16. A contracting unit which has awarded a contract for the provision of wastewater treatment services to a vendor pursuant to this act or the "Local Public Contracts Law," P.L. 1971, c. 198 (C.40A:11-1 et seq.) *may lease* to the vendor, *for a fair market price,* the property to be used as a site for a wastewater treatment system, the provisions of any other laws or rules and regulations adopted pursuant thereto to the contrary notwithstanding.

17. Any contracting unit which, prior to the effective date of this act, has issued a request for qualifications and a request for proposals from vendors for the provision of wastewater treatment services, or has initiated negotiations with a vendor for the provision of wastewater treatment services, may petition the department for certification as being substantially and materially in compliance with the provisions of this act, and, upon receiving this certification, may award a contract for the provision of wastewater treatment services pursuant to the provision of this act.

18. The department and the division may adopt, pursuant to the "Administrative Procedure Act," P.L. 1968, c. 410 (C.52:14B-1 et seq.), rules and regulations necessary to carry out their respective responsibilities under this act.

19. Section 15 of P.L. 1971, c. 198 (C.40A:11-15) is amended to read as follows:

15. Duration of certain contracts. All purchases, contracts or agreements for the performing of work or the furnishing of materials, supplies or services shall be made for a period not to exceed 12 consecutive months, except that contracts or agreements may be entered into for longer periods of time as follows:

(1) Supplying of

(a) Fuel for heating purposes, for any term not exceeding in the aggregate, two years;

(b) Fuel or oil for use of airplanes, automobiles, motor vehicles or equipment for any term not exceeding in the aggregate, two years;

(c) Thermal energy produced by a cogeneration facility, for use for heating or air conditioning or both, for any term not exceeding 20 years, when the contract is approved by the Board of Public Utilities. For the purposes of this paragraph, "cogeneration" means the simultaneous production in one facility of electric power and other forms of useful energy such as heating or process steam.

(2) (Deleted by amendment; P.L. 1977, c. 53.)

(3) The collection and disposal of garbage and refuse, for any term not exceeding in the aggregate, five years;

(4) The recycling of solid waste, for any term not exceeding 25 years, when such contract is in conformance with a solid waste management plan approved pursuant to P.L. 1970, c. 39 (C.13:11E-1 et seq.), and with the approval of the Division of Local Government Services and the Department of Environmental Protection;

(5) Data processing service, for any term of not more than three years;

(6) Insurance, for any term of not more than three years;

(7) Leasing or servicing of automobiles, motor vehicles, machinery and equipment of every nature and kind, for a period not to exceed three years; provided, however, such contracts shall be entered into only subject to and in accordance with the rules and regulations promulgated by the Director of the Division of Local Government Services of the Department of Community Affairs;

(8) The supplying of any product or the rendering of any service

by a telephone company which is subject to the jurisdiction of the Board of Public Utilities for a term not exceeding five years;

(9) Any single project for the construction, reconstruction or rehabilitation of any public building, structure or facility, or any public works project, including the retention of the services of any architect or engineer in connection therewith, for the length of time authorized and necessary for the completion of the actual construction;

(10) The providing of food services to county colleges and county assisted institutions of higher education for any term not exceeding three years;

(11) On-site inspections undertaken by private agencies pursuant to the "State Uniform Construction Code Act" (P.L. 1975, c. 217; C.52:27D-119 et seq.) for any term of not more than three years;

(12) The performance of work or services or the furnishing of materials or supplies for the purpose of conserving energy in buildings owned by, or operations conducted by, the contracting unit, the entire price of which to be established as a percentage of the resultant savings in energy costs, for a term not to exceed 10 years; provided, however, that such contracts shall be entered into only subject to and in accordance with rules and regulations promulgated by the Department of Energy establishing a methodology for computing energy cost savings;

(13) The performance of work or services or the furnishing of materials or supplies for the purpose of elevator maintenance for any term not exceeding three years;

(14) Leasing or servicing of electronic communications equipment for a period not to exceed five years; provided, however, such contract shall be entered into only subject to and in accordance with the rules and regulations promulgated by the Director of the Division of Local Government Services of the Department of Community Affairs.

(15) Leasing of motor vehicles, machinery and other equipment primarily used to fight fires, for a term not to exceed seven years, when the contract includes an option to purchase, subject to and in accordance with rules and regulations promulgated by the Director of the Division of Local Government Services of the Department of Community Affairs.

(16) The provision of wastewater treatment services or the designing, financing, construction, operation, or maintenance, or any combination thereof, on a wastewater treatment system, or any component part or parts thereof, for a period not to exceed 40 years, when the contract for these services is approved by the Division of Local Government Services in the Department of Community Affairs and the Department of Environmental Protection pursuant to P.L. 198, c. __ (C. _____) (now pending before the Legislature as Senate Committee Substitute for Senate Bill No. 991 of 1984). For the purposes of this paragraph, "wastewater treatment services" means any services pro-

vided by a wastewater treatment system, and "wastewater treatment system" means equipment, plants, structures, machinery, apparatus, or land, or any combination thereof, acquired, used, constructed, or operated for the storage, collection reduction, recycling, reclamation, disposal, separation, or other treatment of wastewater or sewer sludge, or for the final disposal of residues resulting from the treatment of wastewater, including, but not limited to, pumping and ventilation stations, facilities, plants and works, connections, outfall sewers, interceptors, trunk lines, and other personal property and appurtenances necessary for their operation.

All multi-year leases and contracts entered into pursuant to this section 15, except contracts for the leasing or servicing of equipment supplied by a telephone company which is subject to the jurisdiction of the Board of Public Utilities, contracts for thermal energy authorized pursuant to [subsection] *paragraph* (1) above, construction contracts authorized pursuant to [subsection] *paragraph* (9) above, [or] contracts and agreements for the provision of work or the supplying of equipment to promote energy conservation authorized pursuant to [subsection] *paragraph* (12) above, *or contracts for wastewater treatment services or for a wastewater treatment system or any component part or parts thereof authorized pursuant to paragraph (16) above,* shall contain a clause making them subject to the availability and appropriation annually of sufficient funds as may be required to meet the extended obligation, or contain an annual cancellation clause.

The Division of Local Government Services shall adopt and promulgate rules and regulations concerning the methods of accounting for all contracts that do not coincide with the fiscal year.

20. This act shall take effect immediately.

5/17/84-R-47

SENATE ENERGY AND ENVIRONMENT COMMITTEE
STATEMENT TO S-991
STATE OF NEW JERSEY
DATED: 5/17/84

Senate Committee Substitute for S-991 establishes a procedure allowing local government units to enter into long-term contracts (up to 40 years) with private firms for the designing, financing, construction, operation, or maintenance of wastewater treatment systems. This procedure would constitute an alternative to any procedure now available.

Under the procedure set forth in this bill, a local government unit would negotiate and award a contract to a private firm for wastewater treatment services in the following manner:

1. Upon deciding to enter into such a contract, the local unit would file a notice of intent with the Department of Environmental Protection, the Division of Local Government Services in the Department of Community Affairs, and the Department of the Public Advocate. This notice would also be published in a local newspaper.

2. The local unit would then issue a request for qualifications from firms interested in contracting to provide the wastewater treatment services. The local unit would review all submitted qualifications, and would establish a list of qualified contractors based on criteria developed by the local unit, including the experience and reputation of the firm.

3. Upon establishing a list of qualified contractors, the local unit requests each qualified contractor to submit a specific proposal, and, upon review of the submitted proposals, the local unit shall negotiate a proposed contract with the contractor submitting the proposal which the local unit determines to be the most advantageous.

4. The local unit conducts a public hearing on the proposed contract. The contractor must be present at the meeting, and the Department of the Public Advocate is authorized to represent the public interest at the meeting and may assess the contractor for the costs incurred in this representation. The local unit shall provide that a transcript of the hearing be printed.

5. After the hearing, the local unit will transmit the proposed contract, a transcript of the public hearing, and a statement discussing the issues raised at the public hearing and the local unit's response to these issues to the Department of Environmental Protection and the Division of Local Government Services. The department will review the proposed contract for its environmental content, and the division will review the contract to [ensure] that it comports with the financial and fiscal capabilities of the local unit. Each agency will have 60 days to approve or conditionally approve the proposed contract.

6. A local unit may award the contract to the contractor only after receiving the approval of the department and the division.

Because the contract will constitute the basis on which the cost of the wastewater treatment service will be calculated, S-991 SCS provides that the contract shall include provisions concerning:

1. The allocation of the risks of financing and constructing the wastewater treatment system.

2. The allocation of the risks of operating and maintaining a wastewater treatment system.

3. The allocation of risks beyond the control of the local unit and the contractor.

4. The defaulting and termination of the contract.

5. The periodic preparation by the contractor of an operating performance report and audited balance statement.

Appendix D

ALABAMA LAW
(Regular Session, 1984)

Act No. 84-314   S.426—Senator Little

AN ACT

To make legislative findings regarding the need to provide additional methods of providing facilities employed in the provision of certain utility services, including water and sewer services, as well as the need for funds to finance such facilities; to define the particular terms used in the subsequent provisions of this act; to provide for and authorize the incorporation by any county or municipality in the state of one or more public corporations and instrumentalities of the state, upon the filing of an application with, and the making of certain determinations by, the governing body of a county or municipality; to provide for and authorize the certificate of incorporation of any such corporation to be amended at any time and from time to time upon the filing of applications with, and the making of certain determinations by, the governing body of such county or municipality; to provide for a board of directors of any such corporation and the election and removal of the members thereof; to authorize any such corporation to acquire, construct, own, lease, make loans with respect to, operate, or enter into contracts for the operation of, facilities, and to provide for the general powers to be exercised by any such corporation and the conditions under which such powers may be exercised; to empower any such corporation to borrow money for its various corporate purposes and in evidence thereof to issue its notes, bonds and other obligations payable solely out of the revenues, receipts, income, funds or other sources specified in the proceedings under which such bonds, notes or other obligations are issued; to authorize any such corporation to pledge its revenues and mortgage or assign its assets as security for its notes, bonds or other obligations; to provide for the issuance of refunding bonds, notes or other obligations by any corporation for the purpose of refunding bonds, notes or other obligations theretofore issued or assumed by it; to provide a method for giving constructive notice of any mortgage, security interest, assignment or pledge created or made by any such corporation; to provide that the notes, bonds or other obligations of any such corporation shall not constitute or create a debt of the state or any county, municipality or other political subdivision or agency thereof; to provide that the notes, bonds and other obligations of any such corporation may be used for the investment of trusts and other fiduciary funds; to exempt from all taxation in the state the property, corporate activities, revenues and income of such corporation, such transaction or actions to which each such corporation is a party or in which it may be involved, and the notes, bonds and all other obligations of each such corporation and the income from such notes, bonds and obligations; to exempt any such corporation from all laws of the state governing usury or prescribing or limiting interest rates; to exempt any such corporation from all laws of the state requiring competitive bids for contracts to be entered into by counties, municipalities or public corporations; to exempt all utility services agreements and other contracts relating to the design, construction, acquisition, financing or operation of facilities financed by a corporation from all laws of the state requiring competitive bids for contracts to be entered into by counties, municipalities or public corporations and all laws relating to the maximum duration of contracts for the sale of personal property and contractual services to counties, municipalities or public corporations; to provide for liberal construction of the provisions of this act; to confer upon any corporation organized under the provisions of this act the power of eminent domain; to exempt any corporation organized under the provisions of this act from state supervision and control; to provide that any county, municipality or other political subdivision, agency or instrumentality of the state or any county or municipality may aid and cooperate with any such corporation, lend or donate money or perform services for the benefit thereof, and, without the necessity of an election, donate, sell, convey, transfer, lease or grant thereto any property of any kind; to authorize any county, municipality or other political subdivision, agency or instrumentality thereof and the Tannehill Furnace and Foundry Commission to enter into utility services agreements, for a term not exceeding forty (40) years, providing for the provision of utility services to such entity by a provider under circumstances in which the facilities for the provision of such utility services are financed, in whole or in part, by a corporation; to provide that such entity may unconditionally and absolutely obligate itself to make payments pursuant to such utility services agreement irrespective of the performance of the facilities or the delivery of the pertinent utility services; to provide that a utility services agreement may provide that when more than one such entity shall be a party to such a utility services agreement and one such entity shall default in its obligations thereunder, then the other such entity or entities may be obligated to assume the payment obligations of such defaulting entity; to provide legal and equitable remedies for the breach of utility services agreements; to prohibit any city, county or instrumentality of either thereof to enter into any utility services agreement or related agreements for the acquisition, construction, equipment or operation of any facilities unless the same shall have been approved by such entity after a public hearing following public notice; to provide that any such corporation shall be a nonprofit corporation; to provide that any such corporation may, in its discretion, publish a notice of the adoption of a resolution authorizing the issuance of bonds, notes or other obligations by such corporation, and to provide that any action or proceeding questioning the validity of any such bonds, notes or other obligations or instruments securing the same must be commenced within thirty (30) days after the first publication of said notice; to provide for the dissolution of any such corporation and for the vesting of title to its properties; and to provide that the provisions of this act shall be severable.

Be It Enacted by the Legislature of Alabama:

Section 1.   Legislative findings: It is hereby found and declared as follows:

(a)   That the health, safety and welfare of the people of this state require the provision of certain utility services, including water and sewer services;

(b)   That it is necessary for the legislature to provide additional methods by which the cities and counties in the state may provide new and improve existing utility services facilities;

(c)   That historically a significant portion of the funding of the costs of construction of such utility services facilities has been provided through grants from the United States of America;

(d)   That, in recent years, funds available to cities and counties from the United States of America for payment of costs of construction of utility services facilities has been substantially reduced, and it is anticipated that, in coming years, such funds may be further reduced or eliminated;

(e)   That the result of the elimination of funding from the United States of America will be to place the entire burden of payment of costs of constructing and improving utility services facilities solely upon the cities and counties in the state;

(f)   That the users of utility services facilities will be forced to pay increased charges in amounts sufficient to enable the cities and counties to provide funds to pay costs of constructing new and improved utility services facilities;

(g)   That it may be impossible for cities and counties to raise rates with respect to the use of such utility services facilities to such levels as will provide funds sufficient to enable such cities and counties to pay substantially all of the costs of constructing and improving such utility services facilities;

(h)   That the legislatures in other states of the United States of America, including surrounding states, have enacted or are considering legislation making available to cities and counties new and different methods of financing the costs of such utility services facilities, to the end that the entire burden of the loss of funds from the United States of America will not be placed directly on the users of such utility services in the form of substantially increased charges;

(i)   That among the alternatives available to cities and counties in the construction of new and improved utility services facilities is the encouragement of private investment in the construction, ownership and operation of utility services facilities;

(j)   That to the extent that the provision of utility services facilities in connection with private ownership and operation reduces the cost of service, the people of this state are greatly benefited by lower cost to the users of such utility services facilities;

(k)   That to the extent that utility services charges in this state are substantially higher than in surrounding states, the industrial development of the state is adversely affected and the improvement of the quality of the environment of the state impeded.

The legislature, therefore, finds and declares that it is necessary, desirable and in the public interest that additional and alternative methods of providing for the construction and improvement of certain utility services facilities be provided; and that the provisions of this act are in the public interest and promote the health, welfare and safety of the citizens of this state.

Section 2.   Definitions. The following words and phrases used in this act, and others evidently intended as the equivalent thereof, shall, in the absence of a clear implication herein otherwise, be given the following respective interpretations herein:

''Applicant'' means a natural person who files a written application with the governing body of any county or municipality in accordance with the provisions of section 3 hereof.

''Authorizing resolution'' means a resolution or ordinance adopted by the governing body of any county or municipality in accordance with the provisions of section 3 hereof, that authorizes the incorporation of a corporation.

"Board" means the board of directors of a corporation.

"Bonds"means bonds, notes or other obligations representing an obligation to pay money.

"Corporation" means any public corporation organized pursuant to the provisions of this act.

"Costs" as applied to a facility or any portion thereof, shall include all or any part of the cost of construction, acquisition, alteration, enlargement, extension, reconstruction, improvement and remodeling of a facility, including all lands, structures, real or personal property, rights-of-way, franchises, easements, permits, approvals, licenses and certificates and interests acquired or used for, in connection with or with respect to a facility, the cost of demolishing or removing any buildings or structures on land so acquired, including the cost of acquiring lands to which such buildings or structures may be moved, the cost of all machinery and equipment, financing charges, underwriters' commissions or discounts, interest prior to, during the following completion of such construction and acquisition, provisions for reserves for both principal and interest and for maintenance, extensions, enlargements, additions and improvements to any facilities then being or theretofore acquired and all other amounts authorized by any corporation to be paid into any special funds from proceeds of bonds issued by the corporation, the cost of architectural, engineering, financial and legal services, plans, specifications, studies, surveys, estimates of cost and revenues, administrative expenses, expenses necessary or incident to determining the feasibility or practicability of constructing a facility and such other expenses as may be necessary or incident to the construction and acquisition of a facility, the financing of such construction and acquisition and the placing of a facility in operation.

"County" means any county in the state.

"Determining county" means, with respect to a corporation, any county the governing body of which shall have made findings and determinations of fact pertaining to the organization of such corporation in accordance with the provisions of section 3 of this act.

"Determining municipality" means, with respect to a corporation, any municipality the governing body of which shall have made findings and determinations of fact pertaining to the organization of such corporation, in accordance with the provisions of section 3 of this act.

"Determining subdivision" means, with respect to a corporation, any determining county or determining municipality and, with respect to an instrumentality, the county or municipality or combination thereof whose governing body is empowered to incorporate or otherwise establish such instrumentality.

"Director" means a member of the board of a corporation.

"Eligibility investment" includes (a) any time deposit with, or any certificate of deposit issued by, (i) any bank which is organized under the laws of the United States of America or any state thereof and deposits in which are insured by the Federal Deposit Insurance Corporation or any department, agency or instrumentality of the United States of America that may succeed to the functions of such corporation or (ii) any savings and loan association which is organized under the laws of the United States of America or any state thereof and deposits in which are insured by the Federal Savings and Loan Insurance Corporation or any department, agency or instrumentality of the United States of America that may succeed to the functions of such corporation; (b) any debt securities that are direct, general obligations of the United States of America; (c) any debt securities the payment of the principal of and interest on which is unconditionally guaranteed by the United States of America; (d) any debt securities that are direct, general obligations of any agencies or instrumentalities of the United States of America, including the following: the Export-Import Banks of the United States, the Federal Farm Credit Banks, the Federal Land Banks, the Federal Intermediate Credit Banks, the Banks for Cooperatives, the Federal Home Loan Banks (including any joint obligations of any two or more of the foregoing agencies), the Federal Home Loan Mortgage Corporation (including participation certificates of the last named agency), the Government National Mortgage Association (including participation certificates of the last named agency), the Tennessee Valley Authority, the Federal Reimbursement Bank and the Farmers Home Administration; (e) any debt securities that are direct, general obligations of the Federal National Mortgage Association; (f) prime commercial paper or finance company paper which is rated not less than prime one or the equivalent thereof by Moody's Investors Service, Inc., or Standard & Poor's Corporation, or their successors; (g) units of investment in any money market fund which is rated not less favorably than A (or the equivalent thereof) by Moody's Investors Service, Inc., or Standard & Poor's Corporation, or their successors; and (h) any debt obligation in which an insurance company organized under the laws of the state may legally invest its money at the time of investment by an authority.

"Facility" means property or collections of property used to provide utility services, including all land, rights-of-way, property rights, franchise rights, buildings and other structures, machinery, equipment, vehicles, furniture, fixtures, reservoirs, wells, intakes, mains, laterals, pipes, aqueducts and all other property, rights, easements and interests necessary or desirable in connection therewith.

"Governing body" means, with respect to a municipality, its city or town council, board of commissioners, or other like governing body exercising the legislative functions of a municipality and, with respect to a county, its county commission or other like governing body exercising the legislative functions of a county and, with respect to an instrumentality or Tannehill Furnace and Foundry Commission, its board of directors or other like governing body duly constituted to exercise the ultimate decision-making functions of such instrumentality or said Tannehill Furnace and Foundry Commission, as the case may be.

"Governmental user" means any county or municipality, or any instrumentality of either thereof (including, without limitation to, any corporation incorporated hereunder) or Tannehill Furnace and Foundry Commission, that receives, participates in or otherwise partakes of utility services pursuant to a utility services agreement.

"Incorporators" means the persons forming a public corporation pursuant to the provisions of this act.

"Instrumentality" means, with respect to any county or municipality, any public corporation, public authority, board, commission or other similar body that is incorporated, established or controlled by such county or municipality.

"Municipality" means an incorporated municipality in the state.

"Person" means any natural person, public or private corporation (including, without limitation to, any corporation incorporated hereunder), partnership, trust, foundation, government or governmental body, political subdivision or other legal entity.

"Provider" means any person that provides utility services to any user pursuant to a utility service agreement.

"Revenues" means all rentals, receipts, income and other charges derived or received or to be derived or received by the corporation, from any of the following: the operation by the corporation of a facility or facilities, or part of either thereof; the sale, including installment sales or conditional sales, lease, sublease, or use or other disposition of any facility or portion thereof; repayment of any loan with respect to any facility or the operation thereof; contracts, agreements or franchises with respect to a facility (or portion thereof); any gift or grant; proceeds of bonds to the extent of use thereof for payment of principal of, interest or premium, if any, on the bonds is authorized by the corporation; proceeds from any insurance, condemnation or guaranty pertaining to a facility or property mortgaged to secure bonds or pertaining to the financing of a facility; and income and profit from the investment of the proceeds of bonds or of any revenues.

"State" means the state of Alabama.

"Tannehill Furnace and Foundry Commission" means the "Tannehill Furnace and Foundry Commission" created under Article 10 of Chapter 9 of Title 41 of Code of Alabama 1975, as amended.

"Utility services" means any services for (i) the collection, treatment and delivery of water, whether such water is used for human consumption or industrial use, and (ii) the collection, treatment and disposal of sewage, wastewater, industrial effluent or other fluid waste.

"Utility services agreement" means any agreement between or among one or more users and one or more providers, whether such agreement is in the form of a lease, a service contract, a contract of sale or in any other form, pursuant to which a provider or providers shall agree to provide one or more utility services to, or for the benefit of, such user or users under circumstances in which the facilities for the provision of such utility services are financed, in whole or in part, by a corporation.

"User" means any person that receives, participates in or otherwise partakes of utility services pursuant to a utility services agreement, and includes any governmental user.

Section 3.   Filing of application for incorporation of a corporation; authorization of incorporation by governing body of county or municipality. A public corporation may be organized pursuant to the provisions of this act in any county or municipality. In order to incorporate such a public corporation, any number of natural persons, not less than three, who are duly qualified electors of the determining county or the determining municipality, as in the case may be applicable, shall first file a written application with the governing body of such county or municipality, which application shall:

(1)   Contain a statement that the applicants propose to incorporate a corporation pursuant to the provisions of this act;

(2)   State the proposed location of the principal office of the corporation;

(3)   State that each of the applicants is a duly qualified elector of the county or the municipality with whose governing body such application is filed; and

(4)   Request that the governing body of such county or municipality adopt a resolution declaring that it is wise, expedient, necessary or advisable that the proposed corporation be formed and authorizing the applicants to proceed to form the proposed corporation by the filing for record of a certificate of incorporation in accordance with the provisions of section 4 hereof.

Every such application shall be accompanied by such supporting documents or evidence as the applicants may consider appropriate. As promptly as may be practicable after the filing of the application with it in accordance with the provisions of this section, the governing body of the county or the municipality with which the application was filed shall review the contents of the application, and shall adopt a resolution either denying the application or declaring that it is wise, expedient, necessary or advisable that the proposed corporation be formed and authorizing the applicants to proceed to form the proposed corporation by the filing for record of a certificate of incorporation in accordance with the provisions of section 4 hereof. The governing body with which the application is filed shall also cause a copy of the application to be spread upon or otherwise made a part of the minutes of the meeting of such governing body at which final action upon said application is taken.

Section 4.   Incorporation procedure: contents execution and filing of certificate of incorporation. (a) Within 40 days following the adoption of an authorizing resolution the applicants shall proceed to incorporate a corporation by filing for record in the office of the judge of probate of the county or one of the counties in which the determining subdivision is located a certificate of incorporation which shall comply in form and substance with the requirements of this section and which shall be in the form and executed in the manner herein provided.

(b) The certificate of incorporate of the corporation shall state:

(1) The names of the persons forming the corporation, and that each of them is a duly qualified elector of the determining subdivision;

(2) The name of the corporation [which shall be "The Governmental Utility Services Corporation of _____," with the insertion of the name of the determining subdivision (which name may include additional wording identifying the region served by the facility), unless the secretary of state shall determine that such name is identical to the name of any other corporation organized under the laws of the state or so nearly similar thereto as to lead to confusion and uncertainty, in which case the incorporators may insert additional identifying words so as to eliminate said duplication or similarity];

(3) The period for the duration of the corporation (if the duration is to be perpetual, subject to the provisions of section 23 hereof, that fact shall be stated);

(4) The name of the determining subdivision together with the date on which the governing body thereof adopted the authorizing resolution;

(5) The location of the principal office of the corporation, which shall be within the boundaries of the determining subdivision;

(6) That the corporation is organized pursuant to the provisions of this act; and

(7) Any other matters relating to the corporation that the incorporators may choose to insert and that are not inconsistent with this act or with the laws of the state.

(c) The certificate of incorporation shall be signed and acknowledged by the incorporators before an officer authorized by the laws of the state to take acknowledgements to deeds. When the certificate of incorporation is filed for record, there shall be attached to it (1) a copy of the application as filed with the governing body of the determining subdivision in accordance with the provisions of section 3 hereof, (2) a certified copy of the authorizing resolution adopted by the governing body of the determining subdivision, and (3) a certificate by the secretary of state that the name proposed for the corporation is not identical to that of any other corporation organized under the laws of the state or so nearly similar thereto as to lead to confusion and uncertainty.

(d) Upon the filing for record of the said certificate of incorporation and the documents required by the preceding sentence to be attached thereto, the corporation shall come into existence and shall constitute a public corporation under the name set forth in said certificate of incorporation. The judge of probate shall thereupon send a notice to the secretary of state that the certificate of incorporation of the corporation has been filed for record.

(e)   The authorization of the incorporation of one corporation shall not preclude the authorization by the governing body of any determining subdivision of the incorporation of other such authorities; provided, that such other corporations shall be required to adopt names or designations sufficient to distinguish them from any corporation theretofore incorporated.

Section 5.   Amendments to certificate of incorporation. The certificate of incorporation of any corporation incorporated under the provisions of this act may at any time and from time to time be amended in the manner provided in this section. The board shall first adopt a resolution proposing an amendment to the certificate of incorporation which shall be set forth in full in the said resolution and which amendment may include any matters which might have been included in the original certificate of incorporation.

After the adoption by the board of a resolution proposing an amendment to the certificate of incorporation of the corporation, the chairman of the board and the secretary of the corporation shall sign and file a written application in the name of and on behalf of the corporation, under its seal, with the governing body of the determining subdivision, requesting such governing body to adopt a resolution approving the proposed amendment, and accompanied by a certified copy of the said resolution adopted by the board proposing the said amendment to the certificate of incorporation, together with such documents in support of the application as the said chairman may consider appropriate. As promptly as may be practicable after the filing of the said application with the governing body of the determining subdivision pursuant to the foregoing provisions of this section, that governing body shall review the said application and shall find and determine whether it is wise, expedient, necessary or advisable for the said amendment to be made. In finding and determining whether it is wise, expedient, necessary or advisable for the said amendment to be made, the said governing body may consider, in conjunction with any other factors it may deem relevant, alternative means of accomplishing any lawful objective or purpose of the said amendment affecting the public interest. If the said governing body finds and determines that it is wise, expedient, necessary or advisable for the said amendment to be made, it shall adopt a resolution declaring that it has reviewed the said application and has found and determined as a matter of fact that it is wise, expedient, necessary or advisable for the said amendment to be made; if the said governing body finds and determines that it is not wise, expedient, necessary or advisable for the said amendment to be made, it shall deny the application. Such governing body shall also cause a copy of the said application and all accompanying documents to be spread upon or otherwise made a part of the minutes of the meeting of said governing body at which final action upon the said application is taken.

Within 40 days following the adoption by the governing body of the determining subdivision of a resolution finding and determining as a matter of fact that it is wise, expedient, necessary or advisable for said amendment to be made, the chairman of the board of the corporation and the secretary of the corporation shall sign, and file for record in the office of the judge of probate with which the certificate of incorporation of the corporation was originally filed a certificate in the name of and in behalf of the corporation, under its seal, reciting the adoption of said respective resolutions by the board and by the said governing body and setting forth the said proposed amendment. If the proposed amendment provides for a change in the name of the corporation, there shall be filed, together with the certificate required by the immediately preceding sentence, a certificate by the secretary of state showing that the proposed new name of the corporation is not identical to that of any other corporation then in existence and organized under the laws of the state or so nearly similar to that of any other such corporation as to lead to confusion and uncertainty. The judge of probate shall promptly examine each such certificate and shall determine whether it is complete and regular on its face and whether the proposed amendment complies with the provisions of this act. If the judge of probate shall find that each such certificate is complete and regular on its face and that the proposed amendment complies with the provisions of this act, he shall require each such certificate to be recorded in the permanent records maintained in his office. Upon the filing of the aforesaid certificates, the said amendment to the certificate of incorporation shall become effective. If the proposed amendment effects a change in the name of the corporation, the judge of probate shall promptly send a notice to the secretary of state, advising him of such change. No certificate of incorporation of a corporation shall be amended except in the manner provided in this section.

Section 6. Board of directors of corporation; election; terms of office; vacancies; qualifications; expenses; impeachment. (a) Each corporation shall be governed by a board of directors. All powers of the corporation shall be exercised by the board or pursuant to its authorization. The board shall consist of three directors who shall be elected by the governing body of the determining subdivision for staggered terms as hereinafter provided. The governing body of the determining subdivision shall specify for which term each director is elected. The initial term of office of one director shall begin immediately upon his election and shall end at 12:01 o'clock, A.M., on January 1 of the first succeeding odd-numbered calendar year following his election. The initial term of office of another director shall begin immediately upon his election and shall end at 12:01 o'clock A.M., on January 1 of the second succeeding odd-numbered calendar year following his election. The initial term of the remaining director shall begin immediately upon his election and shall end at 12:01 o'clock, A.M., on January 1 of the third succeeding odd-numbered calendar year following his election. Thereafter, the term of office of each such director shall be six years. If at any time there should be a vacancy on the board, a successor director to serve for the unexpired term applicable to such vacancy shall be elected by the governing body of the determining subdivision. If the term of office being served by any director shall expire prior to the election of such director for a new term or prior to the election of his successor by the governing body of the determining subdivision, such director shall continue to serve until his successor is elected and qualified, and if such director is elected for a new term after the expiration of the immediately preceding term which he has been serving, his new term of office shall be deemed to have commenced as of the expiration of such immediately preceding term.

(b) Any officer of the determining subdivision shall be eligible for appointment and may serve as a member of the board for the term for which he is appointed or during his tenure as an officer of the determining subdivision, whichever expires first, but he shall not receive a fee for his services; provided, however, that at no time shall the board consist of more than one officer of the determining subdivision. Each director must be a duly qualified elector of the determining subdivision. Directors shall be eligible for re-election. Each director shall be reimbursed for expenses actually incurred by him in and about the performance of his duties. No director shall vote on or participate in the discussion or consideration of any matter coming before the board in which he, his immediate family or any business enterprise with which he is associated has any direct or indirect pecuniary interest; provided, however, that when any such matter is brought before the board, any director having an interest therein which may be in conflict with his obligations as a director shall immediately make a complete disclosure to the board of any direct or indirect pecuniary interest he may have in such matter prior to removing himself and withdrawing from the board's deliberations and vote on the matter presented.

(c)   A majority of the directors shall constitute a quorum for the transaction of business. No vacancy in the membership of the board or the voluntary disqualification or abstention of any member thereof shall impair the right of a quorum to exercise all of the powers and duties of the corporation.

(d)   Any director of the corporation may be impeached and removed from office in the same manner and on the same grounds provided in section 175 of the Constitution of Alabama, or successor provision thereof, and the general laws of the state for impeachment and removal of the officers mentioned in section 175, or successor provision thereof.

(e)   All proceedings of the board shall be reduced to writing by the secretary of the corporation and maintained in the permanent records of the corporation. Copies of such proceedings, when certified by the secretary of the corporation under the seal of the corporation, shall be received in all courts as evidence of the matters therein certified.

Section 7.   Officers of corporation. The officers of a corporation shall consist of a chairman, a vice-chairman, a secretary, a treasurer and such other officers as its board shall deem necessary or appropriate. The offices of secretary and treasurer may but need not be held by the same person. The chairman and vice-chairman of a corporation shall be elected by the board from the membership thereof; the secretary, the treasurer, and any other officers of the corporation may but need not be members of the board and shall also be elected by the board. The chairman, vice-chairman, secretary and treasurer of the corporation shall also be the chairman, vice-chairman, secretary and treasurer of the board, respectively.

Section 8. Powers of corporation; location of facilities of corporation. (a) Every corporation shall have all of the powers necessary and convenient to carry out and effectuate the purposes and provisions of this act, including (without limiting the generality of the foregoing) the following powers:

(1) to have succession in its corporate name for the duration of time (which may be in perpetuity, subject to the provisions of section 22 hereof) specified in its certificate of incorporation;

(2) To sue and be sued in its own name in civil suits and actions and to defend suits against it;

(3) To adopt and make use of a corporate seal and to alter the same at pleasure;

(4) To adopt, alter and repeal bylaws, regulations and rules, not inconsistent with the provisions of this act, for the regulation and conduct of its affairs and business;

(5) To acquire, whether by gift, purchase, transfer, foreclosure, lease or otherwise, to construct and to expand, improve, operate, maintain, equip and furnish one or more facilities, including all real and personal properties that its board may deem necessary in connection therewith, regardless of whether or not any such facility shall then be in existence and, if in existence, regardless of whether or not any such facility is then owned or leased by any person to which such facility may subsequently be sold or leased by such corporation;

(6) To borrow money and to sell and issue bonds as hereinafter provided for any corporate use or purpose;

(7) To lease to any person or persons all or any part of any facility or facilities that are or are to be owned by it, to charge and collect rent therefor and to terminate any such lease upon the failure of the lessee to comply with any of the obligations thereof, all upon such terms and conditions as its board may deem advisable;

(8) To contract to sell, convey of dispose of and to sell, convey or dispose of all or any part of a facility (including but not limited to the

granting of options to purchase a facility to any person), all for such consideration and upon such terms and conditions as its board may deem advisable;

(9) In connection with the financing of the acquisition, construction or operation of one or more facilities, to lend, upon such terms and conditions as its board may deem advisable, all or any portion of the proceeds derived from the issuance of its bonds for one or more or any combination of the following purposes:

(a) To enable such person to borrow an amount not substantially in excess of the equity (determined on any basis not resulting in a higher value for any facility in question that the estimated replacement cost or the appraised market value thereof, whichever may be greater) which such person may then have in any facility or facilities;

(b) To enable such person to refinance any outstanding indebtedness incurred or assumed in connection with the acquisition, improvement or operation of any existing facility or facilities;

(c) To enable such person to finance the costs of acquiring, by purchase, construction or otherwise, one or more facilities and/or the costs of expanding or improving one or more facilities, regardless of whether any such facility has theretofore been owned or leased by such person or is to be acquired or leased by such person; and

(d) To enable such person to borrow working capital for use in the operation of one or more facilities.

(10) To pledge for payment of any bonds issued or assumed by the corporation any revenues from which such bonds are payable as herein provided, and to mortgage or pledge any or all of its facilities or any part or parts thereof, whether then owned or received or thereafter acquired or received, and to pledge any revenues from which such bonds are payable as herein provided as security for the payment of the principal of and the interest and premium, if any, on any bonds so issued and any agreements (including, without limitation, any utility service agreements) made in connection therewith;

(11) To assume obligations secured by a lien on or secured by and payable out of or secured by a pledge of any facility or facilities or part thereof or the revenues derived from any facility or facilities that may be acquired by the corporation;

(12) To make, enter into, and execute such contracts, agreements, leases and other instruments (including, without limitation to, utility service

agreements) and to take such other actions as may be necessary or convenient to accomplish any purpose for which such corporation was organized or to exercise any power expressly granted hereunder;

(13)   To enter into contracts with, to accept aid, loans and grants from, to cooperate with and to do any and all things not specifically prohibited by this act or the Constitution or other applicable laws of the state that may be necessary in order to avail itself to the aid and cooperation of the United States of America, the state or any agency, instrumentality or political subdivision of either thereof in furtherance of the purposes of this act;

(14)   To receive and accept from any source aid or contributions in the form of money, property, labor or other things of value, to be held, used and applied to carry out the purposes of this act, subject to any lawful condition upon which such aid or contributions may be given or made;

(15)   To appoint, employ and contract with such employees and agents, including but not limited to, architects, engineers, attorneys, accountants, financial experts, fiscal agents and such other advisors, consultants and agents as may in its judgment be necessary or desirable, and to fix their compensation;

(16)   To enter into a management contract or contracts with any municipality, any county, or any person or persons for the management, supervision or operation of all or any part of its facilities as may in the judgment of such corporation be necessary or desirable in order to perform more efficiently or economically any function for which it may become responsible in the exercise of the powers conferred upon it by this act.

(17)   To procure insurance against any loss in connection with its property and other assets in such amounts and from such insurers as its board may deem desirable;

(18)   To the extent permitted by the contracts of such corporation with the holders of its bonds and if not otherwise specifically prohibited by any other provision of this act, to invest its moneys (including, without limitation, the moneys held in any special fund created pursuant to any trust indenture or agreement or resolution securing any of its bonds and proceeds from the sale of any bonds) not required for immediate use in eligible investments;

(19)   To include in any borrowing by such corporation such amounts

as may be deemed necessary by its board to pay bond discount, commissions or other financing charges, interest on the obligations issued in evidence of such borrowing for such period as its board shall deem advisable, fees and expenses of financial advisors and planning and management consultants, all legal, accounting, publishing, printing, recording and filing fees and expenses and such other expenses as shall be necessary or incident to such borrowing;

(20)   To the extent permitted by its contracts with the holders of its bonds, to purchase bonds of such corporation out of any of its funds or moneys available therefor and to hold, cancel or resell such bonds;

(21)   To secure payment of bonds or other obligations of such corporation, including performance obligations relating to processes and facilities involved in providing utility services, by procuring or agreeing to procure (i) insurance or guarantees from the United States of America or any agency or instrumentality thereof, or (ii) insurance, guarantees, letters of credit and other sureties from banks, insurance companies and other financial institutions, and to pay premiums, commissions and fees necessary to procure such insurance, guarantees, letters of credit or other sureties;

(22)   To establish and maintain one or more special debt service reserve funds and such other special fund or funds as may be necessary or desirable for its corporate purposes and to pay into each such fund any moneys contributed or granted to such corporation for the purpose of such fund by any governmental or public entity or any private party, any proceeds from the sale of bonds to the extent provided in the resolution adopted by the board of such corporation authorizing the issuance of such bonds and any other moneys which may be made available to such corporation for the purpose of such fund from any other source or sources.

(23)   To require payments in lieu of taxes with respect to any facilities to be made by a provider to the state, a county or a municipality, or any two or more thereof; and

(24)   To do any and all things necessary or convenient to carry out its purposes and to exercise its powers pursuant to the provisions of this act.

(b)   Any facility or facilities of a corporation organized pursuant to determination by a determining municipality may be located within or

without or partially within and partially without the determining municipality, subject to the following conditions:

(1) No such facility or part thereof shall be located more than 30
miles from the corporate limits of the determining municipality;

(2) No such facility or part thereof shall be located within the corporate limits of a municipality other than the determining municipality
in this state unless the governing body of such other municipality has
first adopted a resolution consenting to the location of such facility or
part thereof in such municipality; and

(3) No such facility or part thereof shall be located in a county
other than that (or those) in which the determining municipality (or part
thereof) is situated unless the governing body of such other county has
first adopted a resolution consenting to the location of such facility or
part thereof in such county.

(c) Any facility or facilities of a corporation organized pursuant to
determination by a determining county may be located within or without
or partially within and partially without the determining county, subject
to the following conditions:

(1) No part of a facility shall be located more than three miles
outside the boundaries of the determining county;

(2) In no event shall any facility or part thereof be located within
the corporate limits of a municipality unless the governing body of such
municipality has first adopted a resolution consenting to the location of
such facility or party thereof in such municipality; and

(3) No such project or part thereof shall be located in a county
other than the determining county unless the governing body of such
other county has first adopted a resolution consenting to the location of
a part of such facility in such other county.

Section 9. Bonds of corporation—generally. (a) Any corporation
shall have the power to issue, sell and deliver at any time and from time
to time its bonds in such principal amount or amounts as its board shall
determine to be necessary to provide sufficient funds for achieving any
of its corporate purposes, including the payment of interest on any of its
bonds, the establishment of reserves to secure any such bonds and all
other expenditures of such corporation incident to and necessary or convenient to carry out its corporate purposes and powers. Any corporation

shall also have the power to issue from time to time bonds to renew bonds and bonds to pay bonds, including interest thereon and, whenever it deems refunding expedient, to refund any bonds by the issuance of new bonds, whether the bonds to be refunded have or have not matured, and to issue bonds partly to refund bonds then outstanding and partly for any other of its corporate purposes.

(b) The bonds issued by any corporation shall be authorized by resolution or resolutions adopted by its board, shall bear such date or dates and shall mature at such time or times as such resolution or resolutions may provide, except that no bond shall mature more than 40 years from date of its issue. The bonds of any corporation may be issued as serial bonds or as term bonds or as a combination thereof. The bonds of any corporation shall bear interest at such rate or rates, be in such form and denominations, either coupon or registered, carry such registration privileges, be executed by such officers of such corporation and in such manner, be payable in such medium of payment, at such place or places within or without the state and be subject to such terms of redemption as may be provided in the resolution or resolutions by which they are authorized to be issued. The bonds of any corporation may be sold by such corporation at public or private sale at such price or prices as such corporation shall determine. If such action shall be deemed advisable by the board, there may be retained in the proceedings under which any of such bonds are authorized to be issed an option to redeem all or any part thereof as may be specified in such proceedings, at such price or prices and after such notice or notices and on such terms and conditions as may be set forth in such proceedings and as may be recited in summary form on the face of such bonds; provided that any bond of any corporation having a specified maturity more than 15 years after its date shall be made subject to redemption at the option of such corporation at the expiration of 15 years from its date and on any interest payment date thereafter at such price or prices and after such notice or notices and on such terms and in such manner as may be provided in the resolution adopted by the board of such corporation authorizing the issuance of such bond. Any corporation may pay all expenses, premiums and commissions which its board may deem necessary and advantageous in connection with the issuance of any of its bonds. Issuance by any corporation of one or more series of bonds for one or more purposes shall not preclude it from issuing other bonds, but the resolutions whereunder any subsequent bonds may be issued shall recognize and protect any prior pledge or mortgage made for the benefit of any prior issue of bonds, unless in the proceedings authorizing such prior issue the right was reserved to issue subsequent bonds on a parity with such prior issue.

(c)   Prior to the preparation of definitive bonds, the corporation may issue interim receipts or temporary bonds, with or without coupons, exchangeable for definitive bonds when such bonds shall have been executed and are available for delivery. The corporation may also provide for the replacement of any bonds which shall become mutilated or shall be destroyed or lost.

(d)   All obligations created or assumed and all bonds issued or assumed by any corporation shall be solely and exclusively an obligation of such corporation and shall not create an obligation or debt of the state, the determining subdivision, any other county or, municipality or any other political subdivision of the state or any instrumentality or governmental agency existing under the laws thereof; provided, that the provisions of this subsection shall not be construed to release the original obligor from liability on any bond or other obligation assumed by the corporation.

Section 10.   Security of bonds; contracts and agreements to secure. (a) Bonds issued by any corporation may, as its board may deem advisable, be either general obligations of such corporation or limited obligations payable only out of certain specified revenues or assets of such corporation; provided, that any corporation may enter into contracts with the holders of any of its bonds preventing such corporation from thereafter issuing general obligation bonds or limiting the amount of such bonds that may thereafter be issued. To the extent permitted by any contracts with the holders of outstanding bonds and any other contractual obligations or requirements, any corporation may pledge any of its revenues or mortgage or assign any of its assets, whether real or personal and whether tangible or intangible, to secure the payment of any of its bonds.

(b)   As security for payment of the principal of and the interest and premium, if any, on any bonds issued or assumed by it, any corporation may enter into a contract or contracts, and adopt resolutions or other proceedings containing provisions constituting a part of the contract or contracts with the holders of such bonds, pertaining to, among other things, the following matters:

(1) Pledging all or any part of the revenues of such corporation to secure the payment of such bonds, subject to contracts with the holders of its then outstanding bonds;

(2) Pledging, assigning or mortgaging all or any part of the assets of such corporation to secure the payment of such bonds, subject to contracts with the holders of its then outstanding bonds;

(3) The creation of reserves, sinking funds or other funds and the regulation and disposition thereof;

(4) Limitations on the purpose to which the proceeds of sale of such bonds may be applied and pledging such proceeds to secure the payment of such bonds;

(5) Limitations on the issuance of additional bonds, the terms upon which additional bonds may be issued and secured and the refunding of outstanding bonds;

(6) Binding the corporation to impose and collect reasonable rates for and the imposition of reasonable regulations respecting any service rendered from or with respect to any facility or facilities;

(7) The procedure, if any, by which the terms of any contract with the holders of such bonds may be amended or abrogated, the amount of bonds the holders of which must consent thereto and the manner in which such consent may be given;

(8) Limitations on the amount of moneys to be expended by such corporation for its operating expenses;

(9) Vesting in a trustee or trustees such property, rights, powers and duties as such corporation may determine;

(10) Defining the acts or omissions to act that shall constitute a default in the performance of the obligations and duties of such corporation to the holders of such bonds and providing for the rights and remedies of such holders in the event of such default; provided, however, that such rights and remedies shall not be inconsistent with the general laws of the state and the other provisions of this act; and

(11) Any other matters of like or different character which in any way affect the security or protection of the holders of such bonds.

(c) Any mortgage of property granted by any corporation, any security interest in property created by it or any assignment or pledge of revenues or contract rights made by it, in each case to secure the payment of its bonds, shall be valid and binding from the time when such mortgage is granted, such security interest is created or such assignment or pledge is made, as the case may be, and the property so mortgaged, the property with respect to which such security interest is so created and the revenues and contract rights so assigned or pledged shall immediately (or as soon thereafter as such corporation contains any right thereto or interest therein) be subject to such mortgage, security interest, assignment or pledge, as the case may be, without physical delivery of any property, revenues or contract documents covered thereby or any further act, and the lien of any such mortgage, security interest, assignment or pledge shall be valid and binding as against all persons having claims of any kind in tort, contract or otherwise against such corporation, irrespective of whether such persons have actual notice thereof, from the time notice of such mortgage, security interest, assignment or pledge is filed for record (i) in the office of the judge of probate in which the certificate of incorporation of such corporation was filed for record and (ii) in the case of any mortgage or security interest covering any tangible property, whether real, personal or mixed, in the office of the judge of probate of the county in which such property is or is to be located pursuant to any agreement made by such corporation with any person respecting the location and use of such property. Such notice shall contain a statement of the existence of any such mortgage, security interest, assignment or pledge, as the case may be, a description of the property, revenues or contract rights subject thereto and a description of the bonds secured thereby, all in terms sufficient to give notice to a reasonably prudent person of the existence and effect of any such mortgage, security interest, assignment or pledge. If the requirements of the preceding sentence are met, such notice may consist of (i) a summary statement prepared specially for the purpose of serving as such notice, (ii) an executed counterpart of any mortgage, security agreement, assignment, trust indenture or any other instrument granting such mortgage, creating such security interest or making such assignment or pledge, as the case may be, or (iii) a certified copy of the resolution adopted by the board of such corporation authorizing such mortgage, security interest, assignment or pledge, as the case may be.

(d)   Any corporation shall have power, subject to contracts with the holders of its then outstanding bonds, to purchase for retirement and cancellation any of its bonds and to use any of its available funds for such purpose, provided that, if such bonds are then redeemable, the purchase price thereof shall not exceed the redemption price then applicable, plus accrued interest thereon to the date of purchase, and if such bonds are not then redeemable, the purchase price thereof shall not exceed the redemption price applicable on the earliest date after such purchase upon which such bonds become subject to redemption, plus accrued interest thereon to the date of purchase.

(e)   The bonds of any corporation may, at the discretion of such corporation, be issued under and secured by a trust indenture or trust indentures by and between such corporation and a corporate trustee, which may be any trust company or bank having the power of a trust company within or without the state. Any such trust indenture may contain such provisions for protecting and enforcing the rights and remedies of bondholders as may be reasonable and proper and not in violation of law, including covenants setting forth the duties of such corporation in relation to the exercise of its corporate powers and the custody, safeguarding and application of all moneys. Such authority may provide by any such trust indenture for the payment to the trustee thereunder or other depository of the proceeds of any bonds issued thereunder and any revenues pledged for the security of such proceeds and revenues, with such safeguards and restrictions as it may determine. All expenses incurred in connection with such trust indenture may be treated as part of the operating expenses of such corporation.

(f)   Whether or not the bonds of any corporation are of such form and character as to be negotiable instruments under the terms of the Alabama Uniform Commercial Code, such bonds are hereby made negotiable instruments within the meaning of the Alabama Uniform Commercial Code and for all purposes thereof, subject only to any registration provisions of such bonds. In case any of the directors or officers of any corporation whose signatures appear on any bonds or coupons appertaining to any bond shall cease to be such directors or officers before the delivery of such bonds or coupons, such signatures shall, nevertheless, be valid and sufficient for all purposes to the same extent as if such directors or officers had remained in office until such delivery.

(g)   The directors and officers of any corporation shall not be subject to any personal liability by reason of the issuance of any bonds of such corporation.

Section 11. Proceeds from sale of bonds. All moneys derived from the sale of any bonds issued by a corporation shall be used solely for the purpose or purposes for which the same are authorized; provided, however, that if for any reason any part of such proceeds shall not be necessary for such purposes, then such unexpended part of such proceeds shall be applied to the payment of the principal or of interest on the said bonds. All accrued interest and premium received in any such sale shall be applied to the payment of interest or principal on the bonds sold.

Section 12. Refunding bonds. (a) Any bonds issued or assumed by a corporation may from time to time be refunded by the issuance, by sale or exchange, of refunding bonds payable from the same or different sources for the purpose of paying all or any part of the principal of the bonds to be refunded, any redemption premium required to be paid as a condition to the redemption prior to maturity of any such bonds that are to be so redeemed in connection with such refunding, any accrued and unpaid interest on the bonds to be refunded, any interest to accrue on each bond to be refunded to the date on which it is to be paid, whether at maturity or by redemption prior to maturity, and the expenses incurred in connection with such refunding including, without limitation to, attorneys' fees, costs of printing the refunding bonds, financial advisors' fees and accountants' fees; provided, that unless such bonds are duly called for redemption pursuant to provisions contained therein, the holders of any such bonds then outstanding and proposed to be refunded shall not be compelled without their consent to surrender their outstanding bonds for such refunding. The issuance of such refunding bonds, the maturities and other details thereof, the rights of the holders thereof and the rights, duties and obligations of such corporation in respect thereof shall be governed by the provisions of this act relating to the issuance of bonds generally, to the extent that such provisions may be appropriate therefor.

(b) Refunding bonds issued by any corporation may be sold or exchanged for outstanding bonds issued under this act and, if sold, the proceeds thereof may be applied, in addition to any other authorized purpose, to the purchase, redemption or payment of such outstanding bonds. Pending the application of the proceeds of any such refunding bonds for any of the purposes provided in this section, such proceeds may be invested in any eligible investments pursuant to an escrow agreement providing for the future application of such proceeds in accordance with such purposes.

Section 13.   Freedom of corporation from supervision and control of state; applicability of certain laws regarding operation of facilities. (a) This act is intended to aid the state through the furtherance of the purposes of the act by providing appropriate and independent instrumentalities with full and adequate powers to fulfill their functions. Except as expressly provided in this act, no proceeding, notice or approval shall be required for the incorporation of any corporation or the amendment of its certificate of incorporation, the purchase of any note or other instrument secured by a mortgage, deed of trust, note or other or other security interest, the issuance of any bonds, the execution of any mortgage and deed of trust or trust indenture, or the exercise of any other of its powers by a corporation. Neither a public hearing nor the consent of the state department of finance or any other department, agency, bureau, board of corporation of the state shall be prerequisite to the issuance of bonds by a corporation.

(b)   Each corporation shall, however, be subject to the provisions of the laws of this state respecting the operation of facilities of the corporation, including particularly the provisions of Chapters 23, 25 and 26 of Title 22 of the Code of Alabama of 1975.

Section 14.   Power of eminent domain. Each corporation organized under the provisions of this act is hereby granted the power of eminent domain and may exercise such power in the manner provided by law for the purpose of obtaining real property for any facility or part thereof.

Section 15.   Contacts; cooperation; aid and agreements from other bodies. (a) For the purpose of attaining the objectives of this act, any county, municipality or other political subdivision, public corporation, agency or instrumentality of the state, a county or municipality may, upon such terms and with or without consideration, as it may determine, do any or all of the following:

(1)   Lend or donate money to any corporation or perform services for the benefit thereof;

(2)   Donate, sell, convey, transfer, lease or grant to any corporation,

without the necessity of authorization at any election of qualified voters, any property of any kind; and

(3)   Do any and all things, whether or not specifically authorized in this section, not otherwise prohibited by law, that are necessary or convenient to aid and cooperate with any corporation in attaining the objectives of this act.

(b)   Without in any way limiting the generality of the foregoing, any municipality, county or any political subdivision or agency of the state or of a county or municipality, a public corporation or any other entity is authorized to convey to the corporation, and the corporation in turn is authorized to convey to any person, any existing facility, it being hereby specifically declared that the agreement of any person to whom such conveyance is made to provide a facility or facilities that are in full compliance with all such applicable federal and state laws and regulations shall be deemed to be adequate consideration for any such transfer.

Section 16.   Utility services agreements; incurring indebtedness by governmental users; enforceability of utility services agreements. (a) Any county or municipality, or any instrumentality of either thereof, if authorized by resolution or ordinance of its governing body, may enter into one or more utility services agreements with a provider or providers pursuant to which such provider or providers shall provide one or more utility services for, or for the benefit of, any such governmental user that is a party to such utility services agreement. Any such utility services agreement may provide for the purchase by the governmental user thereunder of all or any part of the capacity, capability or output of the facilities used to provide the applicable utility services. Since the receipt of utility services by a governmental user pursuant to a utility services agreement affords such governmental user the benefits of such utility services without the burdens of ownership and operation of the facilities for the provision of such utility services, and since the payments by such governmental user under such utility services agreement will constitute, in whole or in part, the source of repayment for any financing of the facilities for the provision of such utility services, any utility services agreement may provide (i) that the governmental user thereunder shall be obligated to make the payments required of it by such utility services agreement whether or not the applicable facilities are completed, operable or operating and notwithstanding the suspension, interruption, interference, reduction or curtailment of the capacity, capability or output, as in the case may be applicable, of such facilities or utility services contracted for, the nonperformance or nondelivery of the utility services contracted for, or the inability, for any reason, of the governmental user to receive or partake of the utility services so contracted for, and (ii) that the payments by the governmental user under such utility services agreement shall not be subject to any reduction, whether by offset or otherwise, and shall not be conditioned upon the performance or nonperformance by the provider or providers under such utility services agreement. Any utility services agreement pursuant to which utility services are to be provided to more than one governmental user may also provide that if one or more such governmental users shall default in the payment of its or their obligations thereunder, then in such event the other governmental user or users that are parties to such utility services agreement shall be required to accept and pay for, and shall be entitled proportionately to and may use or otherwise dispose of, the utility services (or the capacity, capability or output thereof) which was to be received by the defaulting governmental user. Any utility services agreement may provide that the obligation of any governmental user to make payments thereunder in respect of utility services shall be as absolute and unconditional as the obligation of such governmental user to repay money that it borrowed directly on its own credit for the purpose of financing the acquisition of facilities that would be used to provide utility services equivalent to those proposed to be provided pursuant to such utility services agreement. Any utility services agreement may extend for a period not exceeding 40 years from the date that such utility services agreement is entered into.

(b)   It is hereby recognized that this act confers upon any governmental user the right to incur payment obligations under a utility services agreement that may constitute debt within the meaning of constitutional limitations and other applicable laws of the state, but, that fact not withstanding, nothing contained in this act shall be construed

(i)   to cause any such debt to lose any exemption from any constitutional debt limit to which, absent any claimed effect of any provision of this act, it would be entitled by virtue of the fact that it was incurred for the purpose of providing waterworks, sewers or sewerage, or

(ii)   to prevent any governmental user from entering into a utility services agreement which provides that payments thereunder due in any fiscal year shall be payable only out of the revenues received by such governmental user during such fiscal year.

(c)   In the event of any failure or refusal on the part of any governmental user to perform punctually any covenant or obligation contained in any utility services agreement, the provider under such utility services agreement shall have the right (i) to recover damages from such governmental user through an action at law or (ii) to enforce performance by such governmental user of such covenant or obligation through any legal or equitable process, including mandamus or specific performance.

Section 17.   Prior Approval of Utility Services Agreements and Related Agreements with Governmental Users; Notice and Public Hearing. (a) No utility services agreement or related agreements in connection with the acquisition, construction, equipment or operation of any facilities may be entered into by any governmental user pursuant to the provisions of this act unless the entering into of such utility services agreement and related agreements by such governmental user is approved by resolution adopted by the governing body of such governmental user in accordance with the provisions of this act; and any utility services agreement or related agreements entered into without prior compliance with the provisions of this section shall be void; provided, however, that no public hearing pursuant to the provisions of this section shall be required in connection with the entering into of any utility services agreement by Tannehill Furnace and Foundry Commission.

(b)   No approval of any utility services agreement or related agreements by the governing body of any governmental user shall be effective for purposes of this act unless such approval is obtained in compliance with the provisions of this section. Prior to entering into any utility services agreement or related agreements, the governing body of any governmental user shall designate a place, date and time at which such governing body shall meet to consider all views expressed by the general public, whether in support or opposition, with respect to such utility services agreement, the utility services to be provided thereunder or any related agreements for the acquisition, construction, equipment or operation of facilities for provision of such utility services. The date of such meeting to hear the views of the general public shall be not less than three weeks after the date on which notice thereof is first published as hereinafter provided. Notice of such meeting shall be published once a week for three consecutive weeks in some newspaper published within the territorial boundaries of such governmental user in the event that the governmental user is a county or municipality, or within the territorial limits of the pertinent determining subdivision or subdivisions in the event that the governmental user is an instrumentality; provided, however, that if no newspaper is at the time being published within the territorial boundaries of such governmental user, or such determining subdivision or subdivisions, as in the case may be applicable, such notice shall be published in a newspaper which the governing body of such governmental user determines to have general circulation within the territorial boundaries of such governmental user or such determining subdivision or subdivisions, as in the case may be applicable; provided further that if no newspaper is at the time being published within the territorial boundaries of such governmental user or such determining subdivision or subdivisions, as in the case may be applicable, and if the governing body of such governmental user determines that there is not newspaper at the time having general circulation within the territorial boundaries of such governmental user or such determining subdivision or subdivisions, as in the case may be applicable, then such notice may be published by posting for three weeks in three public places within such territorial boundaries. Such notice shall be deemed to comply with the requirements of this act if it contains (i) a statement of the intention of the governing body of such governmental user to meet at the designated place, date and time for the purpose of hearing and considering the views of the general public with respect to the approval by such governing body of the entering into of the utility services agreement and related agreements in question, (ii) a brief description of such utility services agreement and related agreements and (iii) the proposed street address of the facilities for the provision of the utility services in question or such other description of the proposed location thereof as will be intelligible to the general public.

At the meeting with respect to which such notice is published, the governing body of the governmental user shall hear and consider the views of all persons desiring to be heard and may thereafter at the same meeting adopt a resolution expressing its final approval or disapproval of the entering into such utility services agreement and related agreements. Instead of taking final action with respect to such utility services agreement and related agreements at the first meeting held to hear the views of the general public, such governing body may defer such action to a subsequent meeting, and it may also continue to hear the views of the general public with respect to such utility services agreement and related agreements during one or more subsequent meetings until it takes such final action, but it may not take any final action with respect to the approval or disapproval of such utility services agreement and related agreements, or conduct other hearings with respect thereto, at any subsequent meeting unless (i) such subsequent meeting is a regular meeting of such governing body or a valid adjournment thereof and (ii) the preceding meeting at which such utility services agreement and related agreements were last considered, such subsequent meeting was publicly designated by such governing body as the place, date and time to which further consideration of such utility services agreement and related agreements was to be continued.

The decision of the governing body of any governmental user to grant or refuse any approval of the entering into of any utility services agreement or related agreements required by the provisions of this act shall be within the sole discretion of such governing body, and, except to the extent affected by fraud, bribery or other unlawful conduct, the reasonableness or fairness of such governing body in approving or refusing to approve the entering into of any such utility services agreement and related agreements shall not be the subject of any case, controversy or inquiry brought before any court of the state.

Section 18. Exemption from taxation, etc. (a) Every corporation shall exercise its powers in all respects for the benefit of the people of the state, for their well being and for the improvement of their health, welfare and social condition, and the exemptions from taxation hereinafter described are hereby granted in order to promote the more effective and economical exercise of such powers.

(b) No income, sales, use or other excise or license tax shall be levied upon or collected in the state with respect to any corporate activities of a corporation or any of its revenues, income or profit. No ad valorem tax or assessment for any public improvement shall be levied upon or collected in the state with respect to any property during any time that title to such property is held by a corporation, including, without limiting the generality of the foregoing, any time that such property is leased to a provider by a corporation pursuant to a lease which provides that title to such property shall automatically pass to such provider upon expiration of the lease term or which gives such provider the right to purchase such property from such authority for a nominal consideration and any time that title to such property is retained by a corporation pursuant to a contract of sale with a provider which provides that title to such property shall not pass to such provider until the purchase price thereof has been paid in full; provided that any corporation may require any provider to pay to such corporation or to any county, municipality or the state payments in lieu of any such ad valorem taxes that would be payable with respect to such property but for the application of the provisions of this section.

(c)   No privilege or license taxes payable in respect of the recording or filing for record of any mortgage, deed or other instrument, including, without limitation, the privilege taxes now imposed by chapter 22 of Title 40, shall be levied, charged or collected in connection with the recording or filing for record of any mortgage, deed or other instrument evidencing a conveyance to or the creation of any property interest in a corporation, any agreement or instrument to which a corporation is a party, and any mortgage, deed or other instrument evidencing a conveyance from a corporation to another party or the creation by a corporation of any property interest in another party.

(d)   If, pursuant to any contractual agreement between a corporation and a provider, any facility has been or is to be acquired by such corporation and leased or sold to such provider or has been or is to be financed by a loan from such corporation, then in such case the gross proceeds of the sale of any property used in the construction and equipment of such facility, regardless of whether such sale is to such corporation, such provider or any contractor or agent of either thereof, shall be exempt from the sales tax imposed by article 1 of chapter 23 of Title 40 and from all other sales and similar excise taxes now or hereafter levied on or with respect to the gross proceeds of any such sale by the state or any county, municipality or other political subdivision or instrumentality of any thereof. Further, if, pursuant to any contractual arrangement between a corporation and a provider, any facility has been or is to be acquired by such corporation and leased or sold to such provider or has been or is to be financed by a loan from such corporation, then in such case any property used in the construction and equipment of such facility, regardless of whether such property has been purchased by such corporation, such provider or any contractor or agent of either thereof, shall be exempt from the use tax imposed by article 2 of chapter 23 of Title 40 and all other use and similar excise taxes now or hereafter levied on or with respect to any such property by the state or any county, municipality or other political subdivision or instrumentality of any thereof.

(e)   All bonds issued by any corporation, their transfer and the income therefrom, including the interest income thereon and any profits made on the sale thereof, shall at all times be free from taxation by the state or any county, municipality or other political subdivision or instrumentality of the state, excepting inheritance, estate and gift taxes.

Section 19.   Exemption from usury and interest laws. Any corporation and all contracts made by it shall be exempt from the laws of the state of Alabama governing unsury or prescribing or limiting interest rates, including, but without limitation to, the provisions of Chapter 8 of Title 8. Further, any payment payable directly or indirectly by any provider pursuant to any lease, installment sale contract, loan agreement or other contract to which a corporation is a party, any payment pursuant to any utility service agreement or any payment pursuant to any other obligation constituting the source of payment for any obligation of a corporation which, in any such case under the laws of the state in effect at the time, constitutes interest, or a payment in the nature of interest, shall be exempt from all such laws of the state governing usury or prescribing or limiting interest rates.

Section 20.   Exemption from competitive bid laws. Any corporation and all contracts made by it shall be exempt from the laws of the state requiring competitive bids for any contract to be entered into by counties, muncipalities, public corporations or other instrumentalities authorized by them, including, but without limitation to, the provisions of article 3 of chapter 16 of Title 41. Further, all contracts, whether or not involving any corporation as a party thereto, which relate to the design, construction, acquisition, financing or operation of any facilities that are financed, in whole or in part, by any corporation pursuant to the provisions of this act (including, without limitation, utility services agreements and contracts for the design, construction and equipment of such facilities) shall be exempt from (i) such laws requiring competitive bids for any contract to be entered into by counties, municipalities, public corporations or other instrumentalities authorized by them, including, but without limitation to, the provisions of article 3 of chapter 16 of Title 41, and (ii) the laws of the state limiting the duration of any contracts for the purchase of personal property or contractual services by counties, municipalities, public corporations or other instrumentalities authorized by them, including, without limitation to, the provisions of article 3 of chapter 16 of Title 41.

Section 21. Disposition of net earnings of corporation. Every corporation shall be a nonprofit public corporation and no part of its net earnings remaining after payment of its expenses shall inure to the benefit of any private person, except that in the event a board shall determine that sufficient provision has been made for the full payment of the expenses, bonds and other obligations of a corporation, then any net earnings of a corporation thereafter accruing shall be paid to its determining subdivision.

Section 22. Bonds of corporation as legal investments. The bonds of any corporation shall be legal investments in which the state and its agencies and instrumentalities, all counties, municipalities and other political subdivisions of the state and public corporations organized under the laws thereof, all insurance companies and associations and other persons carrying on an insurance business, all banks, savings banks, savings and loan associations, trust companies, credit unions and investment companies of any kind, all administrators, guardians, executors, trustees and other fiduciaries, and all other persons whatsoever are now or may hereafter be authorized to invest in bonds or other obligations of the state, may properly and legally invest funds in their control or belonging to them.

Section 23. Dissolution of corporation; vesting of title to corporation's property in determining subdivision. At any time when any corporation has no binds or other obligations outstanding and when there shall be no other obligations assumed by such corporation that are then outstanding, the board of such corporation may adopt a resolution, which shall be duly entered upon its minutes, declaring that the corporation shall be dissolved. Upon filing for record of a certified copy of the said resolution in the office of the judge of probate with which the corporation's certificate of incorporation was filed, the corporation shall thereupon stand dissolved and, in the event it owned any assets or property at the time of its dissolution, the title to all such assets or property shall thereupon vest in the determining subdivision.

Section 24.   Incorporation of another corporation by same determining subdivision. The formation or dissolution of one or more corporations incorporated under the provisions of this act shall not prevent the subsequent incorporation hereunder of other corporations pursuant to authorization by the same determining subdivision.

Section 25.   Notice of bond resolution; contest to validity of bonds, etc. (a) Upon the adoption by the board of any corporation of any resolution providing for the issuance of bonds, such corporation may, in the discretion of its board, cause a notice respecting the issuance of such bonds to be published once a week for two consecutive weeks in each county in which shall be located any facility financed or in any way assisted by the issuance of such bonds, such publication in each such county to be in a newspaper having general circulation therein. Such notice shall be in substantially the following form (the blanks being properly filled in), at the end of which shall be printed the name and title of either the chairman or secretary of such corporation: " _____, a public corporation and instrumentality of the state of Alabama, on the ___day of _____, authorized the issuance of $_____ principal amount of bonds (or notes or other obligations, as the case may be) of the said public corporation for purposes authorized in the act of the legislature of Alabama under which the said public corporation was organized. Any action or proceeding questioning or contesting the validity of the said bonds (or notes or other obligations), or the instruments securing the same, or the proceedings authorizing the same, must be commenced on or before_____(here insert date determined in accordance with the provisions of subsection (b) of this section)."

(b)   The date stated in such notice as the date on or before which any action or proceeding questioning or contesting the validity of the bonds referred to therein must be commenced shall be a date at least 30 days after the date on which occurs the last publication of such notice necessary for it to have been published at least once in all counties in which it is required to be published. Any action or proceeding in any court to set aside or question the proceedings for the issuance of the bonds referred to in such notice or to contest the validity of any such bonds, or the validity of any instruments securing the same, must be commenced on or before the date determined in accordance with the preceding sentence and stated in such notice as the date on or before which any such action or proceeding must be commenced. After such date no right of action or defense shall be asserted questioning or contesting the validity of such bonds, or the instruments securing the same, or the proceedings authorizing the same, nor shall the validity of such bonds or such instruments or proceedings be open to question in any court on any ground whatsoever, except in an action or proceeding commenced on or before such date.

Section 26. Provisions are cumulative. The provisions of this act are cumulative and shall not be deemed to repeal existing laws, except to the extent such laws are clearly inconsistent with provisions of this act.

Section 27. Liberal construction. This act shall be construed liberally to effect its purposes and neither this act nor anything herein contained is or shall be construed as a restriction or limitation upon any powers which any corporation might otherwise have under any laws of the state, and the provisions of this act are cumulative to any such powers.

This act does and shall be construed to provide a complete, additional and alternative method for the doing of the things authorized thereby and shall be regarded as supplemental and additional to other laws. However, the issuance of bonds of any corporation under the provisions of this act need not comply with the requirements of any other law of the state generally applicable to the issuance of bonds, notes and other obligations by other public corporations organized under the laws of the state.

Section 28. Severability. In the event any section, sentence, clause or portion of this act should be declared invalid by any court of competent jurisdiction, such invalidity shall not affect the validity of any of the remaining sections, sentences, clauses or portions of this act, which shall continue effective.

Section 29. Effective date of act. This act shall become effective immediately upon its passage and approval by the Governor, or upon its otherwise becoming a law.

Approved May 16, 1984.

Time: 4:20 P.M.

I hereby certify that the foregoing copy of an Act of the Legislature of Alabama has been compared with the enrolled Act and it is a true and correct copy thereof.

Given under my hand this 21st day of May, 1984.

McDOWELL LEE
Secretary of Senate